CHARACTERS

A ONE-YEAR EXPLORATION OF THE BIBLE THROUGH THE LIVES OF ITS PEOPLE

VOLUME FIVE

JESUS

LifeWay Press • Nashville, Tennessee

Editorial Team, Student Ministry Publishing

Ben Trueblood
Director, Student Ministry

John Paul Basham
Manager, Student
Ministry Publishing

Drew Dixon
Editorial Team Leader,
Content Editor,

April-Lyn Caouette
Production Editor

Matt Atkinson
Art Director

Kaitlin Redmond
Graphic Designer

ISBN: 978-1-0877-0051-9
Item Number: 005823656

Dewey Decimal Classification Number: 242.2
Subject Heading: DEVOTIONAL LITERATURE / BIBLE STUDY AND TEACHING / GOD

Printed in the United States of America

Student Ministry Publishing
LifeWay Resources
One LifeWay Plaza
Nashville, TN 37234-0144

We believe that the Bible has God for its author; salvation for its end; and truth, without any mixture of error, for its matter and that all Scripture is totally true and trustworthy. To review LifeWay's doctrinal guideline, please visit www.lifeway.com/doctrinalguideline.

contents

About Explore The Bible Students

The Whole Truth, For the Whole Student

When it comes to teens, don't avoid the truth. Don't sugarcoat it. *Explore the Bible: Students* helps you present teens with God's Word, allowing for honest and transparent conversations around the Bible as students learn how these ancient words speak into their lives today.

To find out more, go to
goExploreTheBible.com.

How To Use This Study

This Bible study book includes six sessions of content for group and personal study. Regardless of what day of the week your group meets, each session begins with group study. Each group session utilizes the following elements to facilitate simple yet meaningful interaction among students.

INTRODUCTION
This page includes introductory content and questions to get the conversation started each time your group meets.

GROUP DISCUSSION
Continue the group discussion by reading the Scripture passages and discussing the questions on these pages. Finally, conclude each group session with a time of prayer, reflecting on what you have discussed.

BIOGRAPHY
This section provides more in-depth information regarding the biblical character being spotlighted each week and can be included in the group discussion or personal study times.

PERSONAL STUDY
Three personal studies are provided for each session to take students deeper into Scripture and to supplement the content introduced in the group study. With biblical teaching and personal questions, these sections help students grow in their understanding of God's Word and respond in faith.

LEADER GUIDE
A front-and-back Leader Guide for each session is provided on pages 93-104. It can be torn out to use in leading a group. It includes sample answers or discussion prompts to help you jump-start or steer the conversation.

01

introduction

In no other religious writings do we find specific predictions like we find in Scripture—not in the writings of Buddha, Confucius, Mohammed, Lao-Tse, or Hinduism. Yet in Scripture there are well over two thousand prophecies, most of which have already been fulfilled, and many of those relate to Jesus. They tell of His coming, His birth, His suffering, His identity, and His work as Savior and Redeemer.

While Bible scholars debate the exact number, it is safe to say that more than 574 verses in the Old Testament contain direct personal predictions about Jesus, including 65 direct predictions of Jesus' coming. Few will dispute that the Pentateuch alone (the first five books of the Bible) has at least six direct predictions about Jesus: Genesis 3:15; 9:27; 12:2-3; 49:8-12; Numbers 24:15-19; and Deuteronomy 18:15-18. No wonder Jesus rebuked the disciples on the road to Emmaus who were confused about Him on that first Easter Sunday: "'How foolish you are, and how slow to believe all that the prophets have spoken! Wasn't it necessary for the Messiah to suffer these things and enter into his glory?' Then beginning with Moses and all the Prophets, he interpreted for them the things concerning himself in all the Scriptures" (Luke 24:25-27).

People may arrive at various conclusions about who Jesus is, but Scripture clearly identifies Him as the Messiah—the promised One of the Old Testament who would bring salvation.

If you were to interview a random sample of teenagers about what sets Jesus apart from other religious leaders, what responses would you anticipate?

What do you know about Jesus' birth? Why is it important to recognize that this reality was prophesied about hundreds of years before?

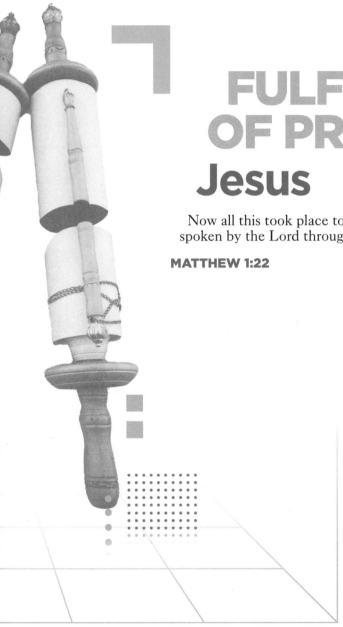

FULFILLMENT OF PROPHECY
Jesus

Now all this took place to fulfill what was
spoken by the Lord through the prophet.

MATTHEW 1:22

// **SON
OF DAVID**

GROUP DISCUSSION

(get started)

focus attention

Share about a time when you had to wait for something important. What was that feeling of waiting like?

GOD WITH US

explore the text

AS A GROUP, READ MATTHEW 1:18-25. */

01 . What is significant about the angel referring to Joseph as "son of David"? What would this have called to mind for Joseph?

02 . Matthew explained that "Immanuel" means "God is with us." What does this phrase teach us about Jesus, and why are these things important?

03 . What do we learn about Joseph from verses 24-25? What must he have believed about Jesus?

AS A GROUP, READ MATTHEW 2:1-8. */

04 . When the wise men arrived in Jerusalem, Matthew said King Herod and all of Jerusalem were "deeply disturbed" (v. 3). What likely caused their reaction?

05 . Look up Micah 5:2-4. What does this tell us about Bethlehem? About Jesus, the Messiah?

AS A GROUP, READ MATTHEW 2:9-12. */

06 . How did the wise men respond to seeing Jesus? Why?

07 . Why do you think the wise men presented Jesus with gifts? How were their gifts connected to their worship?

HE WILL SHEPHERD THEM

apply the text

Since Jesus is both fully human and fully divine, He is qualified to accomplish our salvation and is worthy of our worship—our deepest love, honor, and respect. Jesus fulfilled the Old Testament prophecies, proving that He is the Messiah. God reveals His truth to people who honestly seek to discover that truth. Rejecting Jesus as King doesn't change the fact that He is King.

08 . Both Herod and the wise men had essentially the same facts about the star and the Messiah. Why is intellectual information not enough to cause us to embrace Christ? What else is needed?

09 . Where do you see God at work revealing His plan for redemption in the world today? What role do you see yourself playing in this work?

10 . Jesus' birth shattered religious and cultural barriers. How does He still do this today?

CLOSE YOUR GROUP TIME IN PRAYER, REFLECTING ON WHAT YOU HAVE DISCUSSED. ✱ ⁄

TO FULFILL WHAT WAS WRITTEN

01. _ _ _

02. _ _ _

03. _ _ _

04. _ _ _

05. _ _ _

06. _ _ _

01. _ _ _

02. _ _ _

03. _ _ _

Jesus

THE FULFILLMENT OF PROPHECY

known for

- Jesus was supernaturally born to a Jewish virgin, a fulfillment of Isaiah 7:14 (Matt. 1:22-23; Luke 1:26-38).

- Jesus was born in Bethlehem, a fulfillment of Micah 5:2 (Matt. 2:1,5-6; Luke 2:4,10-11).

- Jesus was born into the lineage of King David, a fulfillment of 2 Samuel 7:12-13; Isaiah 11:1-9; and Psalm 132:11 (Matt. 1:1; Luke 1:32).

- Jesus' birth was preceded by a prophetic forerunner (John the Baptist) announcing His coming, a fulfillment of Isaiah 40:3 and Malachi 3:1; 4:5-6 (Mark 1:1-3).

- Jesus' parents had to flee with Him to Egypt to escape Herod's plan to kill Hebrew babies, fulfilling Jeremiah 31:15 and Hosea 11:1 (Matt. 2:15-18).

- As a young child, Jesus was given tribute and homage as a newborn King, fulfilling Psalm 72:8-11 (Matt. 2:1-2,9-11).

basic facts

- Name Jesus is Greek form of Hebrew name meaning "the Lord saves" or "salvation."

- Eventually became the dividing line of history into BC (Before Christ) and AD (Anno Domini—"in the year of the Lord").

- Actual birth happened around 6–4 BC, before the death of Herod the Great in 4 BC.

04. Birth mother was Mary of Nazareth, a young Jewish virgin engaged to a carpenter named Joseph.

05. Born in Bethlehem in the humblest of settings because Joseph and Mary were required to travel there to register for a census.

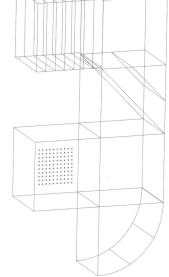

Therefore, the Lord himself will give you a sign: See, the virgin will conceive, have a son, and name him Immanuel.

ISAIAH 7:14

A SIGN

PERSONAL STUDY : 01.

(continue studying on your own)
Read Matthew 1:18-25.

First-century Jewish marriage customs reflected two basic stages of the relationship: the betrothal and the wedding. The young man's parents chose a young woman to be engaged to their son (see Gen. 21:21; 38:6). This sometimes happened when the young men and women were as young as 12–13 years of age. This betrothal was a legally binding contract giving the man legal rights over the woman. This contract could be broken only by a formal process of divorce. Sexual unfaithfulness during this betrothal was considered adultery (which was punishable by death: see Lev. 20:10; Deut. 22:23-24).

01 . What was Matthew trying to explain about the nature of how Mary became pregnant? Why is this so significant for Christianity as a whole?

With discretion, Matthew reported that Mary's pregnancy was discovered before her marriage to Joseph was consummated—meaning they had not yet had sexual relations. The Spirit of God came upon her, and the Child conceived in her womb was divine, human, and sinless. In other words, because Jesus was born of a virgin, He could be fully God and fully man and free of the sin nature that every other human being inherits (Rom. 5:12).

The angel of the Lord is one of God's created beings. The word angel means "messenger," which identified one of an angel's primary roles as a deliverer of God's message to people. An angel named Gabriel appeared in Luke's Gospel to announce the birth of John the Baptist to Zechariah and the birth of Jesus to Mary (see Luke 1:11,19,26). The angel who announced Jesus' birth to the Bethlehem shepherds and to Joseph in his dream is not named.

God sent the angel who appeared to Joseph in a dream to correct him in his dealings with Mary, affirming that her baby's conception was caused by the Holy Spirit. The angel concluded God's message to Joseph by telling him what was to happen with Mary, and what he was to do.

Matthew was careful in his Gospel to show how Jesus fulfilled the prophecies concerning the coming Messiah. This Child born to Mary would be named Immanuel. Jesus means "He saves," and Immanuel means "God with us." He would not be called by this name, but it would describe His role—to be God's presence to people. Jesus literally brought God to earth in a human body. Matthew closed his Gospel with this same promise by quoting Jesus' parting words, in which He promised to be with His followers "always, to the end of the age" (Matt. 28:20).

02 . How do these names, Jesus and Immanuel, complement each other? How does Jesus fulfill both titles?

Matthew was careful to explain that Joseph did not have sex with Mary until after Jesus' birth. He was determined to safeguard the truth that Jesus was conceived and born while Mary was still a virgin. After Jesus was born, Mary and Joseph had many other children, who were Jesus' brothers and sisters (see Matt. 13:55-56). Jesus' siblings did not recognize Him as the Son of God until after the resurrection. Two of His half brothers were instrumental leaders in the early church—James, who was a leader in the Jerusalem church and wrote the Letter of James, and Jude, who authored the New Testament book that bears his name.

PERSONAL STUDY 02.

(continue studying on your own)
Read Matthew 2:1-7.

When these wise men arrived in Jerusalem, they probably expected to find everyone excited about the birth of this Child. They went throughout the city asking about Him. Surely they were shocked that no one seemed to know what they were talking about, even though a general expectation of the coming of a great king and deliverer existed during this time.

01 . What do the questions of the wise men reveal about their expectations? What do your questions about Jesus reveal about your expectations?

Unlike how Luke described an angel appearing to the shepherds (Luke 2:8-15), Matthew did not explain how God revealed to the wise men that the King of the Jews had been born. Instead, He had given them a sign—a star in the sky. Speculation about this star has been widespread. Since Matthew doesn't supply any details about this star, it would be wise to identify it as another miracle surrounding the birth of Christ. This brilliant star followed by the wise men served as God's way to guide them to Jesus. They stated, without apology, that they had come to worship Him, and the worship these men gave to Jesus showed a deeper level of respect than many of His own people gave Him.

02 . What factors contribute to a person's desire to worship God? To what extent are these factors seen in the lives of the wise men?

[the fulfillment of prophecy 15]

Bethlehem ... one will come from you to be ruler over Israel for me ... He will stand and shepherd them in the strength of the LORD... His greatness will extend to the ends of the earth.

Micah 5:2-4

Because of prior invasions, Herod had built several fortresses along the eastern border as protection. Likely, eastern wise men traveled with servants and guards, or even a military escort, to protect themselves as well as the elaborate gifts they were bringing. If such a group had arrived in Jerusalem, Herod would have been informed about it, and he could have considered them part of invading forces coming to join with forces within Israel to dethrone him.

Herod's first response was to gather the chief priests and scribes and inquire of them where the Christ was to be born. He connected the King of the Jews who the wise men were seeking with the Messiah. The religious leaders quickly pointed him to the prophet Micah who, seven centuries before, had given the exact location of the Messiah's birth. In his Gospel, John noted that the Passover crowd in Jerusalem reiterated what the Scriptures stated—the Messiah would come from David's line and from the town of Bethlehem (John 7:42).

Yet these religious leaders did not appear impressed by the wise men's announcement that they had seen the star given as a sign of the Christ's birth. The last phrase of the religious leaders' answer to Herod, describing a leader who would rise to shepherd the people of Israel, was not actually part of Micah 5:2. The popular idea of a shepherd is one who provides kind, tender care (see Ps. 23). Scripture also emphasizes the shepherd's authority and strong leadership. All of these Scriptural facts about the birth of the Messiah were well known. Yet when He came, many of the religious leaders didn't recognize Him and rejected Him.

03 . How did so many of the religious leaders of Jesus' day miss the fact that He was the Messiah? How does the same thing happen today?

PERSONAL STUDY 03.

(continue studying on your own)
Read Matthew 2:8-12.

These wise men from the east were a mystery to Herod. But the most troubling thing of all was the fact they were seeking a Child who they believed had been born King of the Jews.

Herod arranged for a secret meeting. He was not concerned about the meaning or significance of this star they claimed to have followed, just the time that it had appeared. Herod believed that the star that the wise men followed pointed to the birth of someone who could be a threat. If he could learn the time of the star's appearance, he could discover the age of this Child. Herod appeared sincere as he gave the wise men the instructions to continue with their quest to find this Child, and then return and tell him so that he could go and worship the Child also. In his spiritual blindness and hypocrisy, Herod was certain that he had devised a fail-proof plot.

01 . Why might a person view Jesus as a threat today?

God used Herod, a pagan and an enemy of the true God, to give these travelers the directions they needed. As they left Jerusalem, God again resumed His role as their Guide as the star reappeared in the sky. When they were about to continue on their way, they saw that the star had stopped moving. Overwhelmed with joy, they realized that their quest was complete at last!

They reached the house over which the star hovered. When the wise men saw the Child with Mary, they fell to their knees and worshiped Him. These men brought gifts for the infant King. Gold was universally considered a symbol of nobility and royalty. Frankincense was fragrant incense considered a gift for deity (Isa. 60:6), in processions of royalty (Song of Sol. 3:6-7), and occasionally in wedding ceremonies. Myrrh, though not as expensive as frankincense, was nevertheless a valuable fragrance. It was part of the preparation of bodies for burial (John 19:39).

After this time of worship before Jesus, the men left the house. At some point they were warned in a dream not to return to Herod as he had instructed them to do. This divine communication with them was evidence that their role in this event was by God's design.

02 . What do the gifts presented reveal about the identity of Jesus? What do your gifts and worship reveal about your view of Jesus?

02

introduction

Of the four Gospels in the Bible, only two of them talk about the birth of Jesus, but all of them mention Jesus' baptism. Clearly, something very important took place in that moment.

The purpose of John's baptism was to provide an occasion for Jewish people to confess their sins, repent, and also be identified as a people for a coming Messiah based on that repentance, not just their ethnic or religious Jewish identity (Matt. 3:6-11). It was in this context that Jesus approached John, stating that He, too, must be baptized. John didn't understand why. He knew that Jesus didn't have any sin to confess or any sin to repent from.

Jesus' somewhat ambiguous reply acknowledged John's logic, but He nevertheless requested baptism for different reasons. Jesus had not come to confess any sin but "to fulfill all righteousness" (Matt. 3:15). Jesus had previously fulfilled specific prophecies as well as more general scriptural themes. Now He wished to obey all the moral demands of God's will. "To fulfill all righteousness" means to complete everything that forms part of a relationship of obedience to God. In so doing, Jesus identified with and endorsed John's ministry as divinely ordained and his message as one to be heeded.

No wonder, then, the Gospel writers included this in their narratives. For in this moment, Jesus revealed that He performed all the righteousness that would be required of people on their behalf. He showed that He was the Son of God. Jesus joined fallen people, for whom He provides righteousness, by sharing in their baptism.

How would your relationship with God be different if He demanded that you be perfect and repentance wasn't an option?

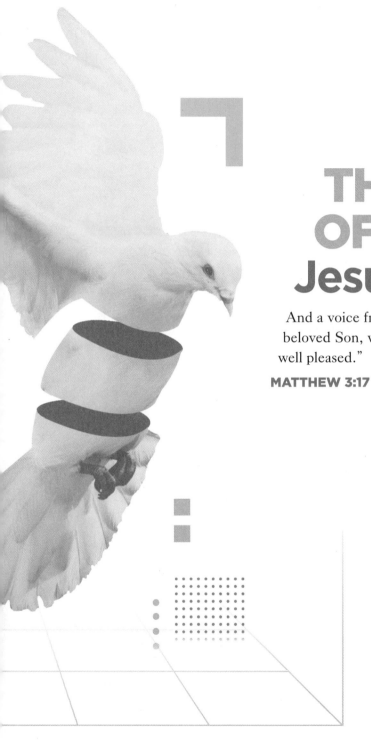

THE SON OF GOD
Jesus

And a voice from heaven said, "This is my beloved Son, with whom I am well pleased."

MATTHEW 3:17

// **A VOICE
CRYING IN THE
WILDERNESS**

GROUP DISCUSSION

focus attention

What are some things you do in order to better identify with someone who is not like you?

PREPARE THE WAY

explore the text

01 . What does it mean to repent? Why did John urge people to repent?

02 . When John told the Pharisees and Sadducees that reliance on Abraham was not enough, how did he point to Jesus?

03 . Why do you think Jesus insisted on being baptized? Why did John hesitate?

04 . Why do you think God's Spirit led Jesus into the wilderness at the very beginning of Jesus' ministry?

05 . Jesus' first temptation is in verse 3. In your own words, what did the devil tempt Him with? What did the devil say about God? How do we face something similar?

06 . In the second temptation, the devil challenged Jesus to jump off the temple. Why was this a temptation for Jesus?

07 . The third temptation involved Jesus being seduced with power. How was this an effort to circumvent God's plans and authority?

08 . How does the temptation of Jesus help us understand His identity?

apply the text

Jesus came to earth as the promised King who provides salvation for those who trust Him. God is at work in our world, unfolding His plans for the redemption of His creation. Christ is all-powerful, bringing salvation for those who trust Him and judgment for those who reject Him. God may use times of temptation to sharpen and shape us. We demonstrate trust in God by standing against the short-term promises of temptation.

09 . Think about some people in your life who need to be told about Christ. Pray for an opportunity to share with them the truths found in this study.

10 . What can you learn from Jesus that will help you face temptation in the future?

11 . How can being involved in a regular study of God's Word help you recognize and deal with temptation?

01. _ _

02. _ _

03. _ _

04. _ _

05. _ _

CLOSE YOUR GROUP TIME IN PRAYER,
REFLECTING ON WHAT YOU HAVE DISCUSSED. ✳✓

01. _ _

02. _ _

03. _ _

**OF THE
LORD**

Jesus
THE SON OF GOD

known for

- Old Testament prophets foresaw the Messiah's divine nature (Isa. 7:14; 9:6-7; Dan. 7:13-14).

- Jesus was conceived supernaturally in the virgin Mary's womb by the Holy Spirit; not conceived by human procreation (Matt. 20-21; Luke 1:35-36).

- Jesus demonstrated sovereign command over both natural and spiritual forces: storms (Matt. 8:23-27; 14:22-33), human diseases and disabilities (Matt. 9:27-31; Mark 5:25-34; Luke 17:11-19), demons (Matt. 9:32-33; Mark 1:23-28), and physical death (Luke 7:11-17; John 11:1-44).

- Jesus claimed to be God in the flesh (Mark 2:6-11; John 5:18; 10:33; 14:1,8-9). Further, He did not reject the assertions of others regarding His deity (John 20:28-29).

- Jesus lived a sinless life (Heb. 4:15), died a voluntary, substitutionary death for others' sins (Rom. 5:6-8; 2 Cor. 5:21), and rose from the dead in victory over both sin and death (Rom. 8:34-39; 1 Cor. 15:20-22).

basic facts

- Second Person of the eternal Trinity.

- Son is equal in nature, essence, and being with Father and Holy Spirit.

- Took on full human nature in incarnation; both fully God and fully human.

04. Divine Agent of creation, redemption of sinners, and restoration.

PERSONAL STUDY 01 .

(continue studying on your own)
Read Matthew 3:1-6.

After describing Jesus' childhood in chapters 1 and 2, Matthew moves ahead more than twenty-five years in chapter 3. John came as a prophet, and Jesus came as the Savior. Both possessed great humility. The people, tired of the cold-heartedness of their religious leaders, were drawn to John's engaging words and responded to his preaching of hope and the coming Messiah. The large crowds followed John, but he still submitted himself entirely to Jesus, noting that he wasn't worthy to remove His sandals (v. 11).

John emphasized repentance in his preaching because the sins of the people alienated them from God. To repent means to do a U-turn from a particular sin or sinful lifestyle that leads away from God's plan for living. The first step in repentance is to admit our sin. Only then will God receive us and give the strength to live according to His law. Signs of repentance include being transparent about our sin, truly remorseful, and consistently working to stop our sinful attitudes and practices. When we sin against other people, repentance requires making things right with the people we have hurt.

Some scholars believe the phrase "the kingdom of heaven" (v. 2) was Matthew's way of respecting the Jewish fear of inadvertently blaspheming the name of God (see Ex. 20:7). Jewish custom did not allow for the proper name of God to be spoken or written. Even today, modern Jews will not write out the name, leaving out some of the letters. John added that the kingdom of heaven had come near. God's kingdom is past, present, and future. God's rule transcends all time. God reigned before Christ came to earth, but when He came, new power was present through Him. This new revelation required people to decide if they would turn and follow God.

01 . What motivates people to present the truth regardless of the reaction of others? How does knowing Jesus is the Son of God give a person confidence to present the truth of the gospel?

Matthew further verified John's identity and earthly mission when he quoted Isaiah's prophecy, claiming that John was the voice crying out in the wilderness and preparing the way for the Lord (see Is. 40:3). Both John and Isaiah taught that repentance is the way to receive God's forgiveness. John was the voice who spoke the message of God.

Repentance is an internal, spiritual act. Many of those in the crowds listening to John were Jewish, so to them baptism was a purification rite for conversion into Judaism. John, however, was using baptism as a sign of repentance. As a result of the conviction of the Holy Spirit, the people confessed their sins, sought God's forgiveness, and were ready to be baptized.

New Testament Christians still practice believer's baptism, which is a symbolic burial of the old self and a rising to walk in newness of life. Baptism happens after one has personally received Christ as Savior. It provides them the opportunity to publicly proclaim their decision to follow Jesus and symbolically identify with Christ's death, burial, and resurrection.

02 . How would you explain the importance of baptism to a person who has never heard of the practice? How does Jesus' baptism help you explain who Jesus is and His purpose in coming to earth?

PERSONAL STUDY 02.

(continue studying on your own)
Read Matthew 3:7-17.

The pious Pharisees and Sadducees were convinced that because they were descendants of Abraham, they were assured God's blessings, regardless of their actions and beliefs. John told them that God could make a nation for Himself from whomever He chose. Matthew saw John's statement as evidence of God's plan to include believing Gentiles among His people. Then John illustrated a principle that has always remained true: just as fruit trees are expected to bear fruit, God's people demonstrate their genuine faith by their good deeds.

The theme of divine judgment surfaced again in John's preaching when he used the analogy of the axe being used to cut down the unproductive trees. John emphasized the complete destruction of these unfruitful trees by noting they would not only be cut down, but would also be thrown in the fire and burned.

01 . What happens to a person's credibility when their words are not followed by sincere and appropriate actions?

John's mission was to prepare the way for the coming of God's Messiah by confronting people with their sins and their need to repent before the Messiah's arrival. Unless the people heeded John's message, they would face the terrifying judgment of a righteous God. John was a beacon used to direct the people beyond himself to the Messiah. He did so with great humility.

Most of those who heard John preach were familiar with threshing floors. The farmer would take a large pitchfork and toss the wheat into the air. The wind would blow through and separate the lighter chaff from the heavier wheat heads. The wheat would be stored to be ground later. The worthless chaff was raked into piles and burned. Winnowing or purging indicated God's judgment upon those who reject His call to repentance. Jesus used this analogy in His

This is my beloved Son

WITH WHOM I AM PLEASED

Matthew 3:17

parable of the wheat and the weeds (see Matt. 13:24-30). John's message was clear: repent, receive Christ, and be saved, otherwise face God's judgment.

02 . How is a Christian's role today different from that of John? How is it similar? How do we point people to Christ today?

Why did Jesus desire baptism? First, with His baptism Jesus endorsed John's ministry. That John was subordinate to Jesus is clear, but that does not lessen the importance of his ministry: John was to call people to prepare for God's Messiah. Second, in being baptized, Jesus identified with the sinners He came to save. Though Jesus was without sin, He related perfectly to the predicament of sinners and died for the sins of all. Third, Jesus was baptized to publicly declare His commitment to follow God's will. He had been relatively unknown until then.

Obedience always brings God's approval. This is represented in three ways immediately following the Son's baptism. First, Jesus glimpsed what He had left, for the heavens were suddenly opened for Him. Second, the descending of the Spirit of God like a dove was a powerful affirmation of Jesus' identity and power. We should not understand from this event that the Spirit was absent from Jesus before that. We should understand it as a spiritual encouragement and empowerment with the deepest of expressions.

The third affirmation of God's approval is the voice from heaven, highlighting the source of unity among the three Persons of the Trinity. That Jesus is the Son supports His identity as the Messiah. The Father was deeply pleased in the obedience of the Son who took on fully the form of a man.

03 . How did the presence of the Father and the Spirit affirm Jesus as being the Son of God? Why was it important for all three to be present?

PERSONAL STUDY 03.

(continue studying on your own)
Read Matthew 4:1-11.

The word tempted simply means "tested." Whether the testing is for good or bad depends on the one giving the test. Satan's intent, obviously, was to lead Jesus to do evil.

The word devil is one of the most common names used for Satan in the Bible. The word means "accuser" or "slanderer." This appearance of Satan shows clearly that he is a personal devil. Because God cast him out of heaven, Satan's fury is aimed in full force against God and His divine mission of salvation.

01 . Why did Jesus intentionally go to the wilderness to face off with Satan?

Mark 1:13 and Luke 4:2 indicate that Jesus was constantly being tempted throughout His wilderness stay. Satan's strategy was likely to wear Jesus down first, before he confronted Him with the specific three temptations. Satan's temptations followed the same pattern used in the garden of Eden and that he continues to use to this day: the lust of the flesh (sexual temptation), the lust of the eyes (coveting), and the pride (desire for power, influence) of life (see 1 John 2:16). Jesus' answer to each temptation was a direct quote from God's Word. All three are found in Deuteronomy.

Satan may have thought he could engage Jesus in a conversation, as he had done with Eve. Jesus simply quoted Deuteronomy 8:3, emphasizing the fact that the Israelites in the desert could not provide bread for themselves and would have to depend on the manna God sent from heaven. Jesus would depend on God to meet His daily needs. Furthermore, Jesus did not live on bread alone but on every word that comes from the mouth of God.

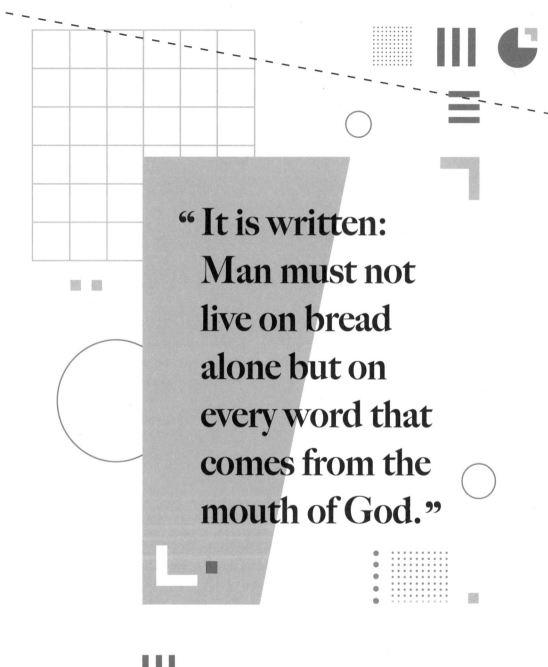

"It is written: Man must not live on bread alone but on every word that comes from the mouth of God."

Matthew 4:4

02 . How does this first temptation serve as an attack against Jesus' identity as Son?

Following this first defeat, Satan took Jesus to the top of the temple in Jerusalem. Again Satan introduced this second temptation with the statement, "if you are the Son of God," seeking to put Jesus on the defensive, as he had done with Eve.

Satan used Scripture to tempt Him (see Ps. 91:11-12). However, he quoted Scripture out of context, making it sound as if God removes the natural consequences of sinful acts. Jesus knew that jumping from the top of the temple would not have been within God's will. The psalm Satan quoted promises God's protection for God's people who are striving to live within His will, yet unintentionally place themselves in danger. God does not promise His protective care for those who deliberately or carelessly place themselves at risk.

Jesus countered Satan's temptation with a quote from Deuteronomy 6:16, which related to an incident during the Israelites' wanderings in the wilderness (see Ex. 17:1-7). The people were without water, and they threatened to abandon Moses and return to Egypt. Moses accused them of testing God and questioning whether He was among them. Indeed Jesus could have jumped from the pinnacle of the temple, and angels would have protected Him from harm. Yet for Jesus to do that would have been a frivolous test of God's power outside His Father's will.

03 . What is the difference between testing God and trusting God? How does Jesus help us understand the difference?

03

introduction

A successful military depends on a clear chain of command. Various symbols of the authority include gestures like snapping to attention in the presence of the commander and quickly offering a salute. Recognition of authority can be heard in the way those of lower rank speak to their superiors. Recognition of authority makes the military run smoothly when commands are given and obeyed.

One of the key aspects of Jesus, Son of God, is His incredible authority. He commands storms to obey, demons to flee, and illnesses to disappear. God's authority is also demonstrated in Scripture, which reveals truth, opens our eyes God's goodness, and has life-giving power when trusted and obeyed. Just as God's spoken word had authority to cause the creation of all things, so God's living Word, Jesus, has authority over all creation. The miracles of Jesus, like his healing of the centurion's servant in Matthew 8, prove that our Savior has authority on a whole other level.

What is the difference between power and authority? Explain.

List some of Jesus' miracles. What do these miracles tell us about Jesus' authority?

THE MIRACLE WORKER
Jesus

When evening came, they brought to him many who were demon-possessed. He drove out the spirits with a word and healed all who were sick.

MATTHEW 8:16

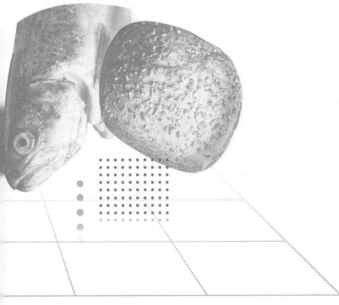

HE DROVE
OUT THE
SPIRITS

GROUP DISCUSSION

focus attention

List stories and movies that include an unexpected plot twist. What makes a plot twist so entertaining?

WITH A WORD

explore the text

AS A GROUP, READ MATTHEW 8:5-7. ✻ ✎

01 . Look at the picture Matthew painted in verses 5-6. What was unusual about this situation?

02 . While the centurion's response unusual, Jesus' response would have been culturally unusual as well. Why? And why was Jesus willing to help?

AS A GROUP, READ MATTHEW 8:8-9. ✻ ✎

03 . What does the centurion's response reveal about this man's understanding of Jesus?

04 . What does Jesus' willingness to go to the centurion's home help us understand about how Jesus valued people?

AS A GROUP, READ MATTHEW 8:10-12. ✻ ✎

05 . What should we make of Jesus' response to the centurion's remarks?

06 . Why was it a big deal that Jesus said what he did about a Roman centurion? What can we learn from this about who we should strive to point to Christ?

AS A GROUP, READ MATTHEW 8:13. ✻ ✎

07 . Jesus demonstrated His authority through the healing of the centurion's servant. What might this mean for our lives?

AND HEALED

(respond to God's Word)

apply the text

Jesus has authority over all creation. When we approach God with a request, we are to do so with confidence in His authority and at the same time with humility. God's authority and ability are not dependent on our faith. Faith in Jesus is the critical requirement for being a part of His kingdom.

08 . How should knowing that Jesus has authority over all things (nature, people, the future, etc.) change how we think of Him? How we live?

09 . Think about some areas of your life are you struggling to recognize Jesus as the authority. What would it take for you to express your dependence on Him in those areas? What keeps you from taking those steps?

CLOSE YOUR GROUP TIME IN PRAYER, REFLECTING ON WHAT YOU HAVE DISCUSSED. ✳✎

ALL WHO WERE SICK

01. _ _

02. _ _

03. _ _

04. _ _

05. _ _

06. _ _

07. _ _

01. _ _

02. _ _

03. _ _

Jesus
THE MIRACLE WORKER

known for

- Changed water to wine at a wedding in Cana (**John 2:1-11**)—revealing His glory as the promised Messiah.

- Healed a royal official's dying son (**John 4:46-54**)—Jesus was in Cana and the sick boy was sixteen miles away in Capernaum. No distance can stop Jesus' healing power.

- Enabled a paralyzed man to walk (**John 5:1-8**)—this miracle sign emphasized the role of trusting and obeying Jesus for healing over human traditions and rules.

- Fed 5,000 people with a boy's lunch (**John 6:1-14**)—Jesus tested His disciples' faith with this miracle and showed the crowd that He was truly the Messiah who provides.

- Walked on water (**John 6:16-21**)—when an evening storm arose, Jesus walked on the sea to the boat to encourage His disciples. Jesus draws near to us.

- Gave sight to a man born blind (**John 9:1-12**)—He revealed that God sometimes uses human disabilities to demonstrate His goodness and glory.

- Raised Lazarus from physical death (**John 11:1-44**)—Lazarus had been dead four days when the Jesus arrived at his tomb. Jesus has power over death.

basic facts

- Miraculously conceived in the virgin Mary's womb.

- Heavenly voice and Spirit's empowerment accompanied His baptism.

- Power to heal and expel demonic spirits was evident early in ministry.

04 . Refused to work miracles simply for popularity's sake.

05 . Opponents falsely accused Him of working miracles by Satan's power.

I am willing.

BE MADE CLEAN

Matthew 8:3

PERSONAL STUDY 01.

(continue studying on your own)
Read Matthew 8:1-4.

Jesus had just presented one of the greatest sermons ever delivered, what we know as the Sermon on the Mount (Matt. 5–7). We can imagine a large crowd assembled and followed Him as a result of that sermon. They heard someone speak with absolute authority. Some followed Jesus because of what He said, while others followed with the hope of seeing Him perform some type of sign. Jesus continued to reveal His authority.

The mention of leprosy would have made the first-century reader gasp. Everyone was terrified of this disease. Anyone who came in contact with a leper was ritually unclean and at risk of his or her life. Lepers were outcasts. They were to stay far away from healthy people and were obligated to warn anyone who might come near (Lev. 13:45-46). This man's willingness to approach Jesus and violate acceptable practice was an expression of his faith. His confident words—not necessarily confidence in Jesus' willingness, but primarily in His ability—further emphasized the man's faith. Addressing Jesus as "Lord" was a way of showing respect.

01. What does the approach of the leper reveal about his understanding of who Jesus was and what Jesus was capable of doing?

Matthew went to great lengths to emphasize Jesus' action. Instead of simply telling us that Jesus touched the man, Matthew explained that Jesus reached out His hand to touch the man. This detail indicates that Jesus took initiative, and that His touch was purposeful. He extended Himself for the benefit of this man in need. Jesus' willingness to touch the leper was an expression of compassion. He could have simply spoken to the man to heal him of the leprosy.

02 . According to Jewish law, touching a leper made a person unclean (See Leviticus 13:1-2,45-46) . Why then did Jesus heal the man by touching him (v. 3)? What does this tell us about Jesus?

Jesus knew exactly what He was doing when He touched the leper. In effect, He would be identified with and treated like the leper. Of course, at Jesus' touch nothing can be defiled. Jesus not only remained clean; He made the unclean clean! Touch in Jesus' ministry is important. Throughout Matthew we see Jesus touching the hand of Peter's sick mother-in-law (8:15), touching a dead body (9:25), and touching a blind man's eyes (9:29). Restoration was a testimony to the power and authority of Jesus as Messiah.

03 . How does Jesus' willingness to touch people impact how you approach Jesus? How does His example impact how you approach others?

Periodically throughout Matthew, Jesus warns people not to spread the word about a miracle they had witnessed (see 9:30; 12:16; 16:20; 17:9). Primarily, this was to keep Jesus' popularity under control until the time was right for His death. He was not hiding from the crowds, but His focus was on training His disciples. Before He was arrested and sentenced to death, Jesus wanted to help His disciples grow.

Jesus' warning to the man also serves to highlight the urgency of going directly to the priest. According to Leviticus 13 and 14, there was a strict procedure for people with skin diseases. It involved periodic inspection by the priests and offering a sacrifice to restore the healed person's clean status before God. Jesus demonstrated respect for the religious practices even when the leaders responsible for those practices rejected Him. Jesus wanted the man to go to the priests at the temple as a testimony to them. These priests would eventually be numbered in the group that led the charge against Him. This man's miraculous recovery from leprosy was to be an indication to the religious leaders that the Messiah had arrived.

PERSONAL STUDY 02.

(continue studying on your own)
Read Matthew 8:5-13.

A Roman centurion who possessed significant authority was desperate. He humbled himself to ask for help from Jesus.

Jesus offered to go to the centurion's home and heal the servant. By doing so, Jesus demonstrated a total lack of prejudice against a Gentile. Furthermore, Jesus voiced a readiness to enter the Gentile's home, something the devout Jewish leaders would have refused to consider.

01 . What role does the centurion's character play in this story? Should it play a role? Explain.

The centurion addressed Jesus as Lord. The Gentile soldier most likely meant the term to carry the kind of respect that a present-day soldier would use in addressing a superior officer. The Jewish elders pleaded for Jesus to help by praising the centurion, saying that he was worthy of Jesus granting his request (see Luke 7:4).

The centurion declared his sense of unworthiness by acknowledging Jesus' far superior authority. He appeared reluctant to ask Jesus to enter his house and deemed it unnecessary. He revealed his belief that Jesus could heal from a distance. Given the observation that no prior instance is recorded of Jesus healing from a distance, the centurion's faith was uncommonly strong.

The centurion gave an explanation of the basis for his confidence in Jesus. He compared Jesus' ability to heal by a word to the authority residing in commands given by a military leader. The centurion knew how to react to those who had authority over him, as well as what it meant to have those under him recognize his authority.

02 . What in Jesus' life gave the centurion reason to believe in Jesus' authority?

The centurion's insight on authority amazed Jesus. Such faith was not usually found in a Gentile. Jesus spoke about others who would come to Him with such faith. Jesus used the imagery of sharing a meal with Abraham, Isaac, and Jacob as a way of expressing the blessedness that came with being included in God's future kingdom. Jews would immediately associate the patriarchs with this future blessedness. The image pointed to the full and equal inclusion of Gentiles in the future heavenly banquet of the Messiah.

Jesus also pointed out that those who thought they should be first in line as children of the kingdom would face outer darkness by rejecting Jesus as Messiah. As descendants of Abraham, they relied on that ancestry as a guarantee of God's favor. Jesus' pronouncement no doubt came across to His Jewish hearers as a shocking revelation.

03 . To what level do you agree with this statement: "Jesus' authority and ability remains intact even when our faith is lacking or imperfect"? Explain.

Having addressed the crowd with His compliment of the centurion's faith, Jesus turned back to him and told him that what he believed had been done. Upon returning home, the centurion found his servant healed. Without ever entering the Gentile's house, healing had occurred in the same moment Jesus had spoken.

PERSONAL STUDY 03.

(continue studying on your own)
Read Matthew 8:14-17.

After telling the stories of an unnamed leper and an anonymous centurion, Matthew included a brief account regarding a family member of one of Jesus' own inner circle. At the time of Matthew's writing, critics might have been able to dismiss these previous two stories. But the naming of a specific person who living eyewitnesses were more likely to back up would silence many of Jesus' critics.

Matthew highlights Jesus' compassion for yet a third category of people who were viewed as second-class citizens within Judaism—women. We also see Jesus' ability to heal a third kind of illness, in this case a fever.

01 . What do we learn about the compassion of Jesus from His interaction with Peter's mother-in-law?

As with the leper, Jesus healed with a touch. Touching women in this fashion was banned by at least some Jewish traditions. Religious leaders seldom touched a woman at all. These men wanted to avoid any possibility of becoming ritually "unclean," so they kept their distance from women.

Like the two previous healings found in Matthew 8, the cure took place at once. Peter's mother-in-law responded by getting up and serving the One who served her. Miraculously, her recovery was so complete that she had the strength to prepare a meal for Jesus. The way Matthew wrote this indicates that the mother-in-law continued to serve. Her action may imply nothing more than proper etiquette as a hostess. But the verb used by Matthew for "serve" eventually came to refer to Christian service. Matthew also pointed out that the healed mother-in-law served Jesus while Mark and Luke note that she served "them" (see Mark 1:31 and Luke 4:39). Using the word "him" may suggest that the woman began a life of discipleship at this point.

02 . How does the response of Peter's mother-in-law demonstrate what she understood about Jesus' source of authority?

From Mark's account, we learn that Jesus healed Peter's mother-in-law on a Sabbath. Jesus had privately done something that would later result in public hostility. Matthew did not note the day of the week here, but the information from Mark explains why people waited until sunset to bring their sick. Sunset marked the end of the Sabbath when normal activity could resume.

Long into the night, Jesus ministered to everyone who came. There was no demon too powerful for Him to remove by simply speaking a word, and no illness too great for Him to heal. Jesus was the sovereign authority over all creation, and He extended Himself sacrificially in compassion to the desperate masses.

Matthew's account reminds readers that Jesus fulfilled the messianic prophecy of Isaiah 53:4. Jesus' fulfillment of this prophecy went far beyond the healing of the body to the healing of the sinful soul. On this earth, God chooses when and how to dispense healing. This verse reminds us that believers should look forward to the banishment of all sickness and death in eternity.

These three specific healings point to Jesus' authority. At the end of chapter 7, Matthew indicated that Jesus also taught with authority (see 7:29). The Greek word used can also be found in Matthew 10:1; 28:18; Mark 1:22,27; Luke 4:36; John 5:27; 10:18; and Revelation 12:10. Matthew makes it clear that Jesus has the authority to do what only God can do because He is God.

03 . Why do the gospels constantly point out Jesus' authority? What is one area of your life you need to submit to Jesus' lordship?

53:4

Yet he himself bore
our sicknesses, and
he carried our pains

ISAIAH 53:4

ISAIAH

AND PAIN

04

introduction

One of the more common terms people used when addressing Jesus was "Rabbi," a term that designated Him as a respected teacher. Jesus employed wisdom sayings, puns, metaphors and proverbs in many of his teaching. He also told stories, asked questions, and connected the dots between Scripture passages. Jesus chose to make simple stories a major feature of His preaching and teaching. We refer to these stories as parables.

Jesus' parables—simple stories that communicate a deeper moral or spiritual lesson—made the truth understandable and memorable. The angled way parables present truth makes them difficult to resist and forces us to explore their meaning and implications for our lives. We are, in effect, invited into the story to find ourselves and live in response to the parable's meaning.

Parables were the most frequent way Jesus explained the kingdom of God, described the character of God, and described the kind of life God wants us to live in the kingdom Jesus was establishing. Matthew 13 serves as an excellent example in this regard. It is fitting introduction to Jesus' teachings. This parable about a sower and the soil describes ways people respond to His teaching.

Recall a story that helps you remember some timeless or important truth. What is the truth, and how does that story help you remember that truth?

What would you expect Jesus to be like as a teacher? How does Jesus' role as a teacher compliment His role as Savior?

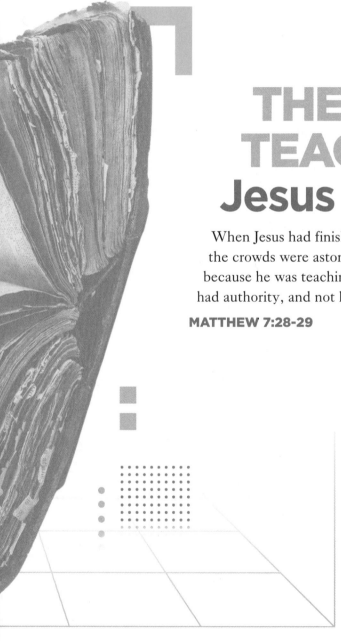

THE MASTER TEACHER
Jesus

When Jesus had finished saying these things, the crowds were astonished at his teaching, because he was teaching them like one who had authority, and not like the scribes.

MATTHEW 7:28-29

THE CROWDS WERE ASTONISHED

GROUP DISCUSSION

focus attention

Why did Jesus tell so many stories? What does that tell us about Him?

HE WAS TEACHING THEM

explore the text

01 . What do these verses reveal about Jesus' heart for people?

02 . How did the story relate to the people who heard Jesus that day? Why was it important for Jesus to help everyone present identify with one of the soils in His story?

03 . What warnings did Jesus give through this parable? How do the warnings given relate to Jesus' identity as the Messiah?

04 . What should we make of the varying amounts harvested in verse 8? What does this reveal about Jesus' value for all people?

05 . What was Jesus' reason for using parables? How did the use of parables serve Jesus' greater purpose?

06 . How does Jesus' response to the disciples' question point to His authority as the Son of God?

07 . How did Jesus' use of parables fulfill Old Testament prophecy? How did Jesus' use of parables confirm Jesus' as the Messiah?

apply the text

Jesus revealed the secrets of His kingdom to His followers. He shared whenever there was a willing group assembled. When the gospel is shared, the response will vary. Everyone should be given the opportunity to hear Jesus' teachings, even those who reject Him.

08 . What is the gospel? How might telling a story help you communicate the gospel to people?

09 . How might we help and encourage one another to share the good news about Jesus with the people around us?

CLOSE YOUR GROUP TIME IN PRAYER, REFLECTING ON WHAT YOU HAVE DISCUSSED. ✳╱

01 . _ _

02 . _ _

03 . _ _

04 . _ _

05 . _ _

01 . _ _

02 . _ _

03 . _ _

AS ONE WITH AUTHORITY

Jesus

THE MASTER TEACHER

known for

"Sermon on the Mount" (Matt. 5–7)—Jesus described key characteristics of God's kingdom and what life in the kingdom He was establishing looks like.

"Mission Discourse" (Matt. 10)—Jesus instructed His twelve apostles on how to take God's kingdom message into Jewish towns.

"Parables Discourse" (Matt. 13)—Seven parables include "the sower," "the wheat and weeds," "the mustard seed," "the leaven," "the treasure in a field," "the priceless pearl," and "the large net."

"Discourse on the Church" (Matt. 18)—Having introduced the idea of the church in 16:18, Jesus instructed the disciples on the importance of ongoing humility, commitment, and forgiveness among believers in the Christian community.

"Olivet Discourse" (Matt. 24–25)—Jesus prophesied that the temple would be destroyed and then taught His disciples what to look for as the sign of His return and the end of the age. He used several parables to emphasize the need for believers to be faithful and alert for His coming.

basic facts

Showed astonishing wisdom and understanding as a twelve-year-old.

Publicly read and explained the Scriptures at His hometown synagogue.

Taught about God's kingdom with unparalleled authority, unlike the scribes of His day who relied on traditions and on quoting the opinions of previous rabbis.

04 . Used effective teaching methods, including parables, question-and-answer conversations, quotation and application of Scripture, mentoring, demonstration, and hands-on practice followed by debriefing.

05 . Was called a "Rabbi" (John 1:49) and "a teacher who has come from God" (John 3:2).

Ask God to help you see the glory of Christ's kingdom and to use you in it.

PERSONAL STUDY 01.

(continue studying on your own)
Read Matthew 13:1-13.

Jesus' often taught in stories called "parables." Parables were simple stories that invited a comparison using images and situations familiar to the listener. Matthew 13 is a major block of teaching composed entirely of parables about the kingdom of heaven, Matthew's preferred term for the kingdom of God. The kingdom of heaven is God's reign (which is one translation of the word "kingdom") or sovereignty.

Teachers usually sat while speaking and their audience stood while hearing, so Jesus sat in the boat to speak to the standing crowd. Even if we were to assume that Jesus left the crowded house in order to find solitude at the seashore, we should take note that whenever a crowd assembled, Jesus was willing to share His message with them.

01 . How would you describe Jesus' willingness to address the crowd? What does His willingness reveal about His concern for all people?

Jesus invoked the image of a typical first-century farmer sowing seed in a field. The crowd would have envisioned a sower with a bag of seeds walking across the field while scattering the seeds. Having covered the field with seeds, the farmer would then likely go back over the field scratching or plowing the seeds into the soil. Jesus focused not on the sower or his seeds, but on the different types of soil found in the field.

There are four different types of soil, and all but one of them refer to people who ultimately reject Jesus as Lord and Savior.

In Jesus' story, the same amount of seed fell on the unfruitful places as fell on good ground, but Jesus emphasized the productivity of good seed planted on good ground. He assigned varying percentages to the potential harvest, some seeds yielding a crop one hundred times more than the volume of seeds sown, others sixty times more, and some thirty times more. While responses to the truths of the kingdom might vary from person to person, they nevertheless heard and understood the message (see 13:23).

02 . Why was Jesus willing to tell parables of His kingdom to people who would not understand them?

03 . Why is it important that we share Christ with people regardless of how we think they will respond?

In responding to the disciples' question about why He spoke to the crowds in parables, Jesus referred to the secrets of the kingdom of heaven. We usually think of secrets as special information we withhold from others. In the New Testament, the idea is different. Sometimes referred to as "mysteries," secrets are truths that can only be known as God reveals them. Truths about God's kingdom come only as He makes them known, as He did through Jesus' ministry of teaching and through inspired prophets and disciples writing other books of the Bible.

The principle behind using parables to reveal truth to committed followers was simply that those with hearts of faith would see how it applies to their lives. They would understand and grow.

Ask God to help you see the glory of Christ's kingdom and to use you in it.

PERSONAL STUDY 02.

(continue studying on your own)
Read Matthew 13:24-33.

The parable of the sower and soils wasn't the only story Jesus told to the crowds. The man who sowed good seed cast the seed broadly. Wheat was not sown in rows but evenly distributed throughout the field.

Under the cover of night and while the owner and workers were sleeping, an enemy could easily slip into the field to cast other seed. Since there were no carefully tilled rows, he could throw the seed just as the original sower did. Roman law included stiff penalties for anyone who would do this, as it ruined people's crops. The success of the crop was essential to the survival of the people, so this act was particularly evil.

The weeds were also called "darnels," and would have grown just like the wheat. This particular weed is practically indistinguishable from wheat in its early growth—only when the weeds matured would they be recognizable. The master knew the source of the bad seed. The enemy was always near and ready to attempt to disrupt his plans. The enemy was successful in introducing the weeds.

01. How would you expect the sower to respond once he discovered the presence of the weeds and the identity of the one who introduced the bad seed?

The master had a greater perspective on the matter and a greater patience. Both the wheat and the weeds were mature plants at this stage, and the roots would have intertwined. Pulling up the weeds would also uproot the wheat. The harvest was the appropriate time for the separation.

The emphasis here is on patience. God is not impulsive. He is able to see the larger picture, and His allowing evil to exist has a purpose. We want to judgment to happen quickly, but this is rash and reckless. It also reflects a lack of compassion. Peter, a disciple known for his reckless and impulsive behavior, also likely would have wanted to immediately eradicate evil. However, his years with Jesus helped him see the wisdom of waiting. In his second letter, Peter reminded his readers that God's patience in bringing an end to evil is motivated by His desire for people to come to repentance (see 2 Pet. 3:9).

02 . How is God's patience a reflection of His wisdom and love for people? How does Jesus' teaching about patience give us insight into Jesus Himself and His mission of providing salvation?

Jesus compared the kingdom of God to a mustard seed and to leaven in bread. As with the parable of the weeds, the focus is on the thing growing, with the listener being struck by the contrast between the beginning and the end product.

Jesus' mustard seed parable encouraged His hearers to keep hoping in the power of God to work through these humble instruments and small beginnings. The yeast pointed to the internal process of rising as opposed to outward, physical organization. His kingdom will grow through an internal, unseen, spiritual dynamic.

The change brought about by the King's coming was not the military and political takeover that most Jews expected. Instead, the change the King caused was one that happened within the inner, unseen person. Jesus' kingdom took spiritual territory away from the unseen enemy. He rescued souls; He did not capture land or seats of political power. Nevertheless, the message of the kingdom would reach the entire world.

PERSONAL
STUDY : 03.

(continue studying on your own)
Read Matthew 13:36-43.

When Jesus dismissed the crowd, the disciples asked Him to explain the parable of the weeds. The gospel always has had an entry-level appeal to all people. All are invited, but those who have accepted Christ as Lord obviously have a greater opportunity to hear and understand His teaching.

In this parable, the emphasis is on two different seeds and the fact that they coexist in the world. That the field is the world is very important in interpreting this parable. Jesus obviously intended the gospel to be taken throughout the world eventually (see Matt. 28:19-20).

The good seed represents the sons of the kingdom. All believers are citizens of the kingdom of heaven. We are part of God's goodness in the world. This great blessing implies great responsibility. The weeds being the sons of the evil one means we live side by side with evil. Christians can't possibly expect to be completely insulated from evil. We don't have the option of locking ourselves away in safety. The separation of good and evil will come in the future. In the meantime, we must be patient with the presence and reality of evil around us.

01 . How does this parable give us a clearer picture of the world in which we live? How does it help us understand the conflicts seen?

The devil has an agenda. He is often ignored and sometimes dismissed as a childish nightmare. The Bible does not allow such indifference. The devil attempts regularly to sow evil, whether in the form of keeping people from the kingdom of heaven or by keeping Christians from growing in Christ. He must

I will open my
mouth in parables;
I will declare things
kept secret from the
foundation of
the world.

Matthew 13:35

not be ignored, nor should he be the focus of too much attention. That the harvest is at the end of the age assures us judgment will come.

The presence of evil is not the final verdict. Judgment delayed is not judgment denied. God has a plan, a purpose, and a timetable that we simply can't know. We must trust that God will bring the world to an end in His time and that evil's reign and damage is both limited and temporary. The coexistence of good and evil in the world may be frustrating to us, but we can trust God to act in His time. At that point we will all be able to see He acted justly and will be grateful our timetable and standards were ignored.

02 . What's wrong with thinking that we have the power to judge others? How does His patience and wisdom make God a worthy judge?

Judgment is God's plan to set all things right. He will renew the world and eradicate from His kingdom everything that causes sin. Evil seems strong and overwhelming at times. We are tempted to wonder if good will win in the end. This parable invites us to trust in God's goodness and plan. In addition to removing the causes of sin, God also will remove those guilty of lawlessness.

The assurance of judgment assures us of two things. It first assures us of the limits of evil. Second, it assures us of the promise of reward. While we are never to serve simply for the rewards, we should remember God does offer an incentive for us to sow good seed. We must take advantage of opportunities to share the good news. We leave judgment to God and are free to live for Him.

03 . How is judgment a function of both love and justice? What does the eventual removal of evil tell us about Jesus' character and purpose?

05

introduction

If you were asked to share one image or symbol that communicates truth about God, what image would you share? As a Christian, that image would almost certainly be a cross. The very place where Jesus appeared to be defeated by death was the very place where victory over death began. In Paul's words, "The word of the cross is foolishness to those who are perishing, but it is the power of God to us who are being saved" (1 Cor. 1:18).

Through His horrific and shameful execution, the guilt of our sin was taken away from us and placed on Jesus, who then released it by His death. By dying in our place for our sins, Christ removed the wrath of God that we justly deserved. Because of our sins, we were alienated—separated—from God. Christ's death removed this alienation and reconciled us to God. Even further, the work of Jesus on the cross redeemed us. He freed us from the power of the curse of the law (Gal. 3:13-14), the guilt of our sin (Rom. 3:23-24), and the power of sin that leads to death (1 Pet. 1:18-19).

When we study Matthew's account of Jesus' sacrificial death on the cross, we are led to worship Him with sincere gratitude. Also, we are moved to serve Him with all our hearts.

What makes the gospel good news?

How does knowing that Jesus died in your place make you feel? How should it shape how we live?

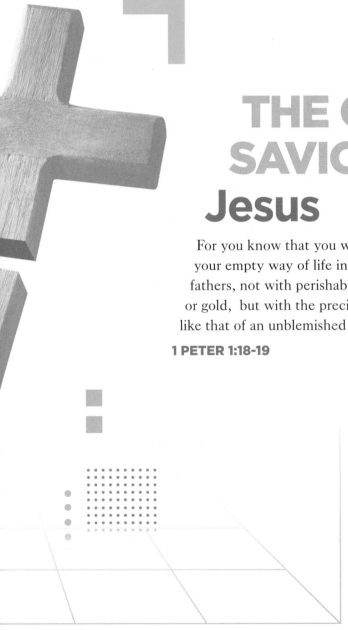

THE CRUCIFIED SAVIOR
Jesus

For you know that you were redeemed from your empty way of life inherited from your fathers, not with perishable things like silver or gold, but with the precious blood of Christ, like that of an unblemished and spotless lamb.

1 PETER 1:18-19

**YOU
WERE
REDEEMED**

GROUP DISCUSSION

(get started)

focus attention

Which of these terms is the most impactful on you personally: mocked, forsaken, or sacrificed? Explain.

FROM YOUR EMPTY WAY

explore the text

01 . Of those who mocked Jesus, who surprises you most?

02 . In what ways were the crowds' taunts and mocking wrong or unfair?

03 . What is the significance of the supernatural events accompanying Jesus' death?

04 . How did Jesus' words reflect His anguish? The pain of sin? His separation from the Father?

05 . Matthew noted that Jesus gave up His spirit. What does that mean, and why is it important for us to understand?

06 . What events marked Jesus' death? How would you interpret the significance of each event?

07 . How should we live in light of Jesus' sacrifice for us?

WITH THE PRECIOUS BLOOD

apply the text

Jesus willingly sacrificed His life to pay the price for all humanity's sin. All of creation, knowingly and unknowingly, testifies to Jesus' being the Messiah. Sin causes separation from the holy God. Jesus' death removed the barrier between God and sinful humanity, making it possible for humans to have an eternal relationship with God through faith in Jesus.

08 . With your group, list ways of testifying that Jesus is the Messiah. What can we do as individuals? What can we do as a group?

09 . Take time to reflect on your life when you were separated from God. What image from the crucifixion best illustrates your life at that time?

10 . Consider the changes that have happened in your life as a result of what Jesus did on the cross and your trust in Him. How has He changed your heart and character?

CLOSE YOUR GROUP TIME IN PRAYER, REFLECTING ON WHAT YOU HAVE DISCUSSED. ✳╱

01 . _ _

02 . _ _

03 . _ _

04 . _ _

05 . _ _

06 . _ _

01 . _ _

02 . _ _

╱╱ **OF CHRIST**

Jesus

THE CRUCIFIED SAVIOR

known for

- Bearing sin's curse (Deut. 21:23; Gal. 3:13; 2 Cor. 5:21)—Paul interpreted Jesus' crucifixion as bearing the law's curse against sin.

- Sacrifice of atonement (Lev. 16:29-30; Heb. 9:24-26)—According to Eph. 1:7, Christ's death provided redemption by offering us forgiveness.

- Jesus is the "propitiation," or atoning sacrifice, for our sins (Heb. 2:17; 1 John 2:2; 4:10).

- Confirmation of the new covenant (Jer. 31:31-34; Luke 22:20)—Jesus' blood established the new covenant promised in the Old Testament (1 Cor. 11:25).

- Jesus is the one who bring redemption and forgiveness to all who believe (Heb. 9:15).

- Embodiment of perfect love (Ex. 34:6-7; Rom. 5:6-10)—showing us how to love others (John 3:16; Rom. 5:8; 1 John 4:10).

basic facts

- Romans perfected crucifixion as a form of execution of slaves, criminals, and enemies of the state.

- Designed to inflict maximum pain, exposure, humiliation to the victim, and deterrence to onlookers; death came slowly after hours or even days of suffering.

03. Foreseen by Jesus as the means by which He would die.

04. Jewish officials would not execute by crucifixion; required official Roman participation.

05. Jesus was crucified despite being guiltless of crimes or sins.

PERSONAL STUDY 01.

(continue studying on your own)
Read Matthew 27:35-44.

Crucifixion typically involved nails being driven through the victim's wrists and ankles. This form of execution was terribly cruel and painful. While the Roman empire was innovative in many ways, it was also incredibly brutal—this was, in part, how Rome managed to conquer most of the known world. Roman soldiers were professional killers, and crucifixion duty would not have pricked their consciences in the least. They would strip and nail a man to a cross and then divide His clothes by casting lots at the foot of the cross, paying no attention to the repulsive nature of such a scene.

Guarding Jesus there may have been a special assignment because of His fame and the fear that the people might try to free this prisoner. More likely, however, the soldiers guarded every prisoner to prevent any possibility of escape.

> **01 .** Why did Jesus have to suffer such a cruel and painful death on the cross? How should the nature of His death impact your attitude toward Jesus?

Often the Romans would nail a list of crimes over the head of the accused. In Jesus' case this wooden board bore the words, "This is Jesus, the King of the Jews." In other words, they accused him of inciting a revolt against Rome. Possibly the Romans were simply making a cruel joke. It is unlikely that they actually took Jesus seriously as a political threat. However, this accusation, from the Roman perspective, is the one that would have legitimately led to Jesus' death. Even so, Pilate was didn't really want to pass this sentence. He recognized this was a power play among ever-feuding Jews. While Jesus was not the kind of king they feared He was, He was and is King in a far more important and profound way.

02 . In what way were the words on the sign accurate? What kind of king is Jesus?

After the soldiers nailed Jesus to the cross, people passing by hurled insults at Him. The religious leaders took advantage of the opportunity to insult Jesus too.

The leaders ridiculed Jesus because they didn't think He could save Himself. They recalled His ministry among them and the way He had delivered countless people. He had healed diseases, cast out demons, and even raised people from the dead. On the cross, however, He appeared to be completely helpless. Yet for Jesus, saving Himself meant that He wouldn't be able to save sinners. Therefore, He refused to save Himself.

The religious leaders aimed their cruelest taunt at Jesus' relationship with the Father. As He languished on the cross, the religious leaders sneered at the idea that God would rescue Him. They implied that God would not rescue His servants if they had failed to please Him. They insisted that God refused to take pleasure in Jesus because He claimed to be God's Son.

03 . What different types of pain and suffering did Jesus face? Of these types of pain, which do you think was most difficult to endure? Explain.

04 . What do we learn about Jesus from His willingness to go through with the crucifixion?

Jesus faced physical pain, emotional pain (the taunts of the crowd), and spiritual pain (punishment for sin) on the cross. Jesus had the power to stop this but He chose not to. He submitted to the Father's will out of love for Him and love for us.

My God, my God, why have You abandoned Me?

Matthew 27:46

PERSONAL STUDY 02.

(continue studying on your own)
Read Matthew 27:45-49.

They nailed Jesus to the cross in the midmorning. At noon, a blanket of darkness began to shroud the entire area and covered the land until three in the afternoon. This was not normal. For Jewish people in those days, darkness usually represented judgment (see Amos 8:9-10). The religious leaders probably assumed that the darkness underscored God's judgment against Jesus. However, God's judgment was actually directed at the sin of the whole world. Creation responded to God's judgment with darkness.

01 . What do the three hours of darkness teach us about the nature of sin? How is the darkness of sin expressed today?

Pay close attention to Jesus' response to God's judgment on sin. At about three in the afternoon, Jesus exhibited the agony of God's judgment on our sin. In that moment, He cried out in sheer torment over the reality that He bore the sin of all people everywhere. As Jesus cried out the first verse of Psalm 22, He referred to His Father as "Elí" (Matt. 27:46). The name meant "my God." By shouting that name, Jesus demonstrated His relationship with God even as He endured the agony of feeling abandoned.

02 . According to what Jesus cried out on the cross, the separation He felt on the cross was the most painful aspect of His suffering. What does that tell you about Him? About His love? About His mission?

Matthew didn't try to explain what Jesus meant with His cry. He only shared the words that Jesus cried out from the cross. Then he went on to share the response of the people who heard what Jesus had shouted. Instead of understanding that Jesus had called out to God (Elí), they made the mistake of thinking that He was calling for Elijah. Some of the Jewish people in those days believed that Elijah would come to the rescue of God's servants when they were in trouble or danger. That notion appeared to color their thoughts as they tried to understand Jesus' words.

One of the people who stood nearby sprang into action once he heard what Jesus had shouted. He got a sponge that he put on the end of a reed. He soaked the sponge in sour wine and lifted it up to Jesus' mouth. Offering Jesus a drink of the sour wine from the sponge may have been an act of compassion. Or it might have been an attempt to keep Jesus alive and suffering just a little longer. That's possible in light of what the rest of the people said as they waited to see what would happen next to Jesus. Because they thought Jesus called for Elijah, they hoped to catch a glimpse of the famous prophet if he appeared to give Jesus some relief. If Elijah showed up to save Jesus from His torment, they would be able to get a look at him. As Jesus bore the sin of the whole world on the cross, they looked on as if they were watching the latest viral video.

03 . People have a range of reactions when they consider the gruesome way Jesus died. What is your reaction to Jesus' death?

04 . How should Jesus' willingness to suffer and die in this way change what you value? How you live?

PERSONAL STUDY 03.

(continue studying on your own)
Read Matthew 27:50-56.

Ready to complete His assignment of dying for our sins, Jesus shouted again with a loud voice and gave up His spirit. He said, "It is finished," and then He died (John 19:30). The predictions of the prophets—the Son of Man's ministry on earth, His sufferings, and His crucifixion—were once and for all fulfilled. With Jesus' last breath, the redemption of the world was accomplished. With that fulfillment, Jesus willingly gave up His Spirit for the sins of the world.

Notice that death didn't overtake Him unexpectedly like an armed robber would overcome a helpless victim. Instead, Jesus set the exact time when He would give up His life as a sacrifice for sin. When the right time came, He "gave up His spirit." Criminals nailed to crosses lingered sometimes for days before they finally died. But Jesus died within six hours after they nailed Him to the cross. Because He was sovereign, He exercised complete control.

01. How does knowing that He was the one who decided when He died support the teaching that Jesus is the Son of God?

Jesus died at "three in the afternoon" (v. 45). That was the time of the regular afternoon sacrifices at the temple. Therefore, the priests would have been at the temple. Once each year, on the Day of Atonement, the high priest passed through the curtain into the holy of holies and made atonement for the sins of God's people (see Lev. 16:16-28). At the moment Jesus died on the cross, the curtain of the sanctuary was torn in two from top to bottom. Only God could have ripped the curtain from the top down. No other explanation would be sufficient. With the curtain split, God declared that a new day had arrived. The days of the high priests' pleading for God's people came to an end. Because of Jesus' death, sinners had open and direct access to God.

At the very moment that the curtain was being torn in two, something else happened. God's creation punctuated the death of His Son with an earthquake. Matthew pointed to the similarity between the quaking of the earth and the splitting of the curtain. Just like the curtain was ripped in two, the rocks were split as well.

What happened at the tombs also confirmed the powerful impact of Jesus' death. When Jesus took His last breath, tombs were opened. The open tombs didn't reveal the bones of dead people. Instead, the tombs displayed Jesus' power over death. Matthew wrote that many bodies of the saints who had fallen asleep were raised. When he referred to "saints," he had Old Testament believers in mind. They had died but were raised from the dead when Jesus died. The scene provided a forecast into what would happen next. Jesus also would be raised from the dead. The grave would not hold Him. In due time, He would be liberated from it. As a result, resurrection would be a certainty for believers as well (1 Cor. 15:20-22).

02 . What conclusions can be drawn from what happened immediately after Jesus died? How does the impact of what happened continue to be experienced today?

The spectacular signs of the earthquake and all that happened had their intended effect on the centurion as well as the other soldiers who were present. Those pagan soldiers knew little of the Jewish faith. They probably didn't realize the implications of the titles thrown at Jesus when the observers taunted Him. But they knew what a god was. And they knew that the Jews believed in a single, all-powerful God. They also knew the implications of a Son of God enough to proclaim the title with awe at the supernatural wonders they saw at the death of Jesus.

06

introduction

Think about the kinds of things you tend to celebrate and how you tend to celebrate them. Our celebrations may focus on significant people who have made a huge difference in our lives (Christmas, Martin Luther King Jr. Day). Or we may celebrate events that have changed the direction of our lives in a powerful way (graduations, anniversaries, birthdays). Celebrations give us an opportunity to relive life-changing moments so we won't forget them. It can also allow us to express our gratitude for the people who shaped our lives.

On Easter Sunday, Christians celebrate Jesus' victory over death. His resurrection serves as the centerpiece of a believer's relationship with Him. He's alive, and He lives in us the moment we welcome Him into our hearts. Because Christ's resurrection has made an eternal difference to us, the Gospel accounts of Jesus' resurrection deserve our attention. These accounts provide the details surrounding the world-changing moment when Jesus was raised from the grave in defeat of sin and death. As we study it, we're prompted to join followers around the world who worship the living Lord. The account also reminds us that the truth of Christ's resurrection needs to be shared with everyone everywhere.

Recall the last time you celebrated something. What was it and why was it important for you to be a part of that celebration?

How does the resurrection serve as proof that Jesus is the Messiah who came to save His people?

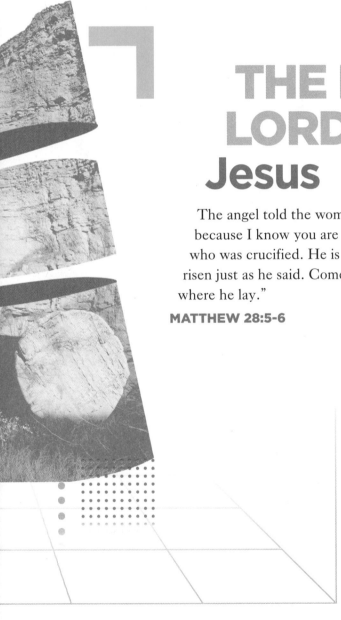

THE RISEN LORD
Jesus

The angel told the women, "Don't be afraid, because I know you are looking for Jesus who was crucified. He is not here. For he has risen just as he said. Come and see the place where he lay."

MATTHEW 28:5-6

DON'T BE AFRAID

GROUP DISCUSSION

(get started)

focus attention

Have you ever witnessed a car accident or crime? Were you asked to report what you saw? Why is eyewitness testimony so important?

**HE IS
NOT
HERE**

explore the text

AS A GROUP, READ MATTHEW 28:1-4. ✳/

01 . What is significant about who discovered the empty tomb?

02 . How does the reaction of the soldiers demonstrate the power of God's glory?

AS A GROUP, READ MATTHEW 28:5-10. ✳/

03 . What evidence of the resurrection do we see in these verses?

04 . Why is it important that we not delay in obeying God?

AS A GROUP, READ MATTHEW 28:11-15. ✳/

05 . What were the motives of the chief priests as they devised their deceptive plan?

06 . What do most people think about the resurrection of Jesus today?

AS A GROUP, READ MATTHEW 28:16-20. ✳/

07 . How did seeing the resurrected Christ change the disciples' view of Jesus?

08 . How is the command that Jesus gave tied to His resurrection?

**FOR HE
HAS
RISEN**

apply the text

Jesus was resurrected to reign forever as the King. Jesus conquered death, affirming His identity and giving all believers hope. As the resurrected King, Jesus is worthy of our worship. Even when faced with the undeniable facts of Jesus' resurrection, some will refuse to believe in Him.

09 . How does Jesus' resurrection give hope?

10 . What role does worshiping Jesus play in your weekly schedule? What adjustments do you need to make to be more involved in worshiping Him?

11 . Think of some people in your life who have not yet accepted Jesus and the truth of the resurrection. How can you lovingly challenge their views and talk to them about the hope you have in Jesus?

CLOSE YOUR GROUP TIME IN PRAYER, REFLECTING ON WHAT YOU HAVE DISCUSSED. ✳╱

**COME
AND
SEE**

01 . __ __

02 . __ __

03 . __ __

04 . __ __

05 . __ __

06 . __ __

01 . __ __

02 . __ __

Jesus

THE RISEN LORD

known for

- The risen Christ appeared first to certain women who believed in Him (Matt. 28:8-10; Mark 16:9; John 20:14-18).

- He appeared to and talked with two followers walking to Emmaus who did not recognize Him as the risen Christ until He hosted their evening meal (Luke 24:13-32).

- Christ appeared to His gathered disciples on several occasions before His ascension (Matt. 28:16-20; Mark 16:14; Luke 24:36-49; John 20:19-23,26-29; 21:1-23).

- The risen Christ appeared in a blinding light to Saul of Tarsus (Paul) on the road to Damascus (Acts 9:3-6).

- The earliest Resurrection Sunday appearances—Matthew 28, Mark 16, Luke 24, and John 20 each open with the arrival of the women (including Mary Magdalene) at the tomb.

- Paul included a summary statement in 1 Corinthians 15:3-7 that provides information about these appearances and others unrecorded in the Gospels or Acts.

basic facts

- Raised others from physical death during His life on earth (Matt. 9:18,23-26; John 11:43-44); these resurrections were temporary—the people later faced physical death again.

- Jesus' resurrection overcame not only the power of physical death but also the power of sin to kill and destroy.

03 . His resurrection leads to eternal life, not merely restored physical life.

04 . The Christian hope of the gospel depends on the reality of the resurrection; without it we are without hope and still in our sins.

He is not here.
For He has
risen, just as He
said. Come and
see the place
where He lay.

Matthew 28:6

PERSONAL STUDY 01.

(continue studying on your own)
Read Matthew 28:1-10.

As soon as the Sabbath came to a close, two women went to Jesus' tomb. Mary Magdalene was a loyal follower of Christ who had looked on in sorrow as He died on the cross. Another woman named Mary accompanied her. Matthew wrote that she was the mother of two of Jesus' disciples (see 27:56). Both of the women had followed along and watched as Jesus' body was removed from the cross and taken to the tomb (see 27:61). They knew where Jesus' body had been laid, and they waited for the Sabbath day to end so they could return.

The angel went to the tomb and opened it. Once he moved the stone from the entrance to the tomb, he sat on it. Notice that he didn't move the stone so Jesus could get out of the tomb. Rather, he moved it out of the way so everyone could get into the tomb and see that Jesus was not there.

The presence of the angel shook the guards. These were tough Roman soldiers who had probably been in battle more than a few times. Yet they were shaken by fear when they saw the angel's radiant splendor. The shock of what they saw overwhelmed them, and they passed out, falling unconscious to the ground. Anyone who saw their helpless figures would have drawn the conclusion that they had died.

01 . How would you explain the contrast between the women and the soldiers? How were their experiences similar? How were their experiences different?

The presence of the angel frightened the women too, but he comforted them. The angel shared with them the reason they couldn't find Jesus' body in the tomb. He encouraged the women to look into the tomb if they needed further confirmation of Jesus' resurrection. The angel didn't want them to be left with any doubt about what had taken place. Jesus had overcome death; He was alive!

02 . What was the significance of the angel inviting the women to see where Jesus had been? Why is the bodily resurrection of Jesus so important to the Christian faith?

The angel gave the women a critical assignment. He directed them to go to the disciples with the message about Jesus' resurrection. The disciples needed to know that He had risen from the dead, and they also needed to know about a meeting Jesus planned to have with them in Galilee. At the moment, they were still in Jerusalem. As soon as they received the message from the women, they needed to make their way to Galilee where they would see Jesus. He would be waiting for them.

Notice that the angel instructed the women to go quickly. They followed his instruction and left in a hurry with a mixture of fear and great joy in their hearts. The women had no idea that they would meet Jesus as they raced to tell the disciples. Hearing Him say "Greetings!" came as a welcome surprise. Once they recognized Him, they immediately worshiped Him. They displayed their submission to Him by bowing before Him and taking hold of His feet. By worshiping Him, they affirmed that He was God. By allowing them to worship Him, Jesus made the same affirmation.

Jesus repeated the assignment that the angel had given to the women, and He urged them not to be afraid as they carried it out. Jesus referred to the disciples as His brothers. The term "brothers" paints an intimate portrait of spiritual kinship. It sheds light on the way Jesus felt about His disciples. He loved them. He looked forward to seeing them in Galilee. Obviously, He wanted to be with them and renew their fellowship. He also wanted to prepare them for the kingdom work ahead of them.

03 . How does Jesus' designation of His disciples (who had earlier abandoned Him) as "brothers" encourage you?

PERSONAL STUDY 02.

(continue studying on your own)
Read Matthew 28:11-15.

At about the same time, guards who had encountered the angel at the empty tomb hurried to Jerusalem too. But they didn't go to Pilate with a report of what had taken place. Instead, they went to the temple and reported to the chief priests what they had seen. They gave their account of the earthquake, the angel who moved the stone, and the empty tomb.

After the priests heard the guards' report, they convened a meeting to discuss how to handle the situation. The news of Jesus' resurrection would turn the world upside down. In doing so, the priests would lose their control over the people of Israel. For that reason, they set out to stifle the report. First, they bribed the guards with a large sum of money. If the guards' superior officers found out about the bribe, the guards would probably have faced execution. In order to take such a big risk, the bribe had to be substantial. Obviously the priests didn't have a problem with bribing the guards. Earlier they had paid Judas thirty pieces of silver so he would betray Jesus (see 26:14-16).

Then the priests made up a story to cover up what had actually happened. Of course, the story didn't make sense. They expected everyone to believe that the troubled band of disciples could actually succeed in a plot to sneak away the body of Jesus in the night, maneuvering around trained Roman soldiers who all just happened to be asleep at the same time.

In their plan to cover up the truth about Jesus' resurrection, the priests anticipated that the guards would need some assurance that they would be protected. The priests assured them that they would not get into trouble with the governor if he found out what had actually happened at the tomb. The priests told the guards to leave the work of persuading Pilate to them. Dealing with him probably involved bribing him too, in order to secure his silence.

The guards agreed to carry out the plan hatched by the priests. Over time, the story spread throughout the land. Their lie prevented some people at that time from believing the truth about Jesus' resurrection.

01 . How would you respond to someone who claimed that Jesus did not actually rise from the dead?

The story that Jesus' disciples had stolen His body and staged His resurrection was one that continued long after it was first told. Matthew penned this Gospel more than twenty years after the resurrection (some scholars estimate that it was at least forty years later), so the lie was still being spread then.

Many people still deny Christ's resurrection. What these people cannot deny are the effects of the resurrection on the lives of those who have been changed by the risen Christ. Skeptics have tried to explain it away for centuries, but when all is said and done, the only real conclusion is that Jesus is alive.

One evidence that points to Christ being raised from the dead is the faith of those who have been transformed by Him. They have a different character than those who do not claim to have Christ indwelling them.

It cannot be explained away with different theories of how the early church tried to concoct a story of such magnitude. One of the challenges of the present-day church is that its people must allow Christ such control of their lives that the world cannot deny them; the evidence of change in Christian lives is just too powerful to overcome.

02 . What are some ways the resurrection should change our lives—the way we think, how we respond to anxiety, how we treat others?

03 . How is your life different now because Jesus really did rise from the dead?

PERSONAL
STUDY 03.

(continue studying on your own)
Read Matthew 28:16-20.

The disciples traveled to Galilee in keeping with the directions Jesus gave them. Before His crucifixion, He told them to meet Him in Galilee after His resurrection (see 26:32). Of course, going to Galilee meant that they would be leaving Jerusalem and the Judean region. It also meant leaving behind the strict religious order established by the Jewish leaders. Things would be different in the kingdom of God that Jesus had established. The established Jewish leaders rejected Jesus as the Messiah. Citizens of the kingdom of God, however, embraced Jesus. Through Him came the joy of a personal relationship with God.

As soon as they saw Jesus, they worshiped Him. Their worship was an expression of devoted reverence. No other response to being in His presence would have been appropriate. Matthew went on to write that some of the disciples doubted. In other words, certain disciples hesitated. The events leading up to their visit on the mountain with Jesus had been difficult to take in. Some of the disciples weren't sure about how they should react to it all.

01 . How is doubt possible after worshiping the resurrected Christ? Why is it important that we identify and express our doubts today?

Jesus made His way toward them. He didn't command them to come closer to Him. Neither did He tell them off because some of them doubted. Jesus began assuring them of His complete authority. By asserting His authority, Jesus assured His disciples that He had the proper justification for giving them orders. Also, He had the ability to give them what they needed so they could carry out His orders successfully. By saying that He had all authority, Jesus reminded His disciples of the reach of His sovereign reign. It extended from earth to heaven. His infinite authority had no boundaries.

The authority Jesus asserted didn't come His way because He took it for Himself. His authority had been given to Him. In order to grasp what Jesus meant, consider Daniel 7:13-14. In that Old Testament prophecy, the Son of Man would be given complete authority by the Ancient of Days to reign over an eternal kingdom. The prophecy painted a picture of God giving all authority to His Son. As Jesus talked with His disciples on the mountain, He assured them that God had given Him all authority to rule over a divine kingdom that would never end.

Growing believers today live in light of the absolute authority of Jesus. We can live in the confidence that He has every right to direct our lives. His authority gives Him the right to commission us to take the gospel to all people. He is able to give us everything we need to serve Him confidently. His authority comes from the reality that He is God.

02 . Why would it have been important for the disciples to understand the greatness of Jesus' authority? Why is it important for you today?

His disciples could go confidently into all the world and make disciples in His name. Before they met Jesus on the mountain, they may have been thinking about staying put or hiding out for a while. Jesus' command wouldn't allow them to consider either an option. They were directed to march ahead with confidence and determination.

No matter what else we may do in our lives, our highest priority is to carry out Jesus' mission wherever we go. Such a mission can become overwhelming, but we aren't alone as we seek to make disciples. We can count on His presence and the help of other believers as we take the good news about Him to the whole world. When we remember His promise to be with us, courage replaces fear as our trust in Him grows stronger.

03 . What is the relationship between Jesus' promised presence and making disciples? How does Jesus' promised presence serve as an encouragement to believers?

MAKE DISCIPLES

"Go, therefore, and make disciples of all nations, baptizing them in the name of the Father and of the Son and of the Holy Spirit, teaching them to observe everything I have commanded you. And remember, I am with you always, to the end of the age."

MATTHEW 28:19-20

28:19-20

IN THE NAME OF THE FATHER

28:19-20

BAPTIZING THEM

TIPS FOR LEADING A SMALL GROUP

Follow these guidelines to prepare for each group session.

Prayerfully Prepare

REVIEW

Review the weekly material and group questions ahead of time.

PRAY

Be intentional about praying for each person in the group. Ask the Holy Spirit to work through you and the group discussion as you point to Jesus each week through God's Word.

Minimize Distractions

Create a comfortable environment. If students are uncomfortable, they'll be distracted and therefore not engaged in the group experience. Plan ahead by considering these details:

SEATING

TEMPERATURE

LIGHTING

FOOD OR DRINK

SURROUNDING NOISE

GENERAL CLEANLINESS

At best, thoughtfulness and hospitality show students they're welcome and valued in whatever environment you choose to gather. At worst, people may never notice your effort, but they're also not distracted. Do everything in your ability to help students focus on what's most important: connecting with God, with the Bible, and with one another.

Include Others

Your goal is to foster a community in which people are welcome just as they are but encouraged to grow spiritually. Always be aware of opportunities to include any students who visit the group and encourage group members to invite their friends. An inexpensive way to make first-time guests feel welcome or to invite someone to get involved is to give them their own copies of this Bible study book.

Encourage Discussion

A good small-group experience has the following characteristics.

EVERYONE PARTICIPATES

Encourage everyone to ask questions, share responses, or read aloud. Since some students may not read as well as others, don't call on students to read out loud—ask for volunteers.

NO ONE DOMINATES—NOT EVEN THE LEADER

Be sure that your time speaking as a leader takes up less than half of your time together as a group. Politely guide discussion if anyone dominates.

NOBODY IS RUSHED THROUGH QUESTIONS

Don't feel that a moment of silence is a bad thing. People often need time to think about their responses to questions they've just heard or to gain courage to share what God is stirring in their hearts.

INPUT IS AFFIRMED AND FOLLOWED UP

Make sure you point out something true or helpful in a response. Don't just move on. Build community with follow-up questions, asking how other people have experienced similar things or how a truth has shaped their understanding of God and the Scripture you're studying. Students will be less likely to speak up if they fear that you don't actually want to hear their answers or that you're looking for only a certain answer.

GOD AND HIS WORD ARE CENTRAL

Opinions and experiences can be helpful, but God has given us the truth. Trust God's Word to be the authority and God's Spirit to work in people's lives. You can't change anyone, but God can. Continually point students to the Word and to active steps of faith.

HOW TO USE
THE LEADER GUIDE

Prepare to Lead

Each session of the Leader Guide is designed to be torn out so you, the leader, can have this front-and-back page with you as you lead your group through the session.

Focus Attention

These questions are provided to help get the discussion started. They are generally more introductory and topical in nature.

Explore the Text

Questions in this section have some sample answers or discussion prompts provided in the Leader Guide, if needed, to help you jump-start or steer the conversation.

Apply the Text

This section contains questions that allow group members an opportunity to apply the content they have been discussing together.

Biography

This section isn't covered in the Leader Guide and may be used during the group session or by group members as a part of the personal study time during the week. If you choose to use them during your group session, make sure you are familiar with the content and how you intend to use it before your group meets.

leader guide
session 1

Focus Attention

Share about a time when you had to wait for something important. What was that feeling of waiting like?

- Israel's period of waiting for the Messiah would soon be over. The King who was promised them so many years before was about to arrive. However, just like today, that first Christmas was filled with surprises.

Explore The Text

ASK A VOLUNTEER TO READ MATTHEW 1:18-25.

01. What is significant about the angel referring to Joseph as "son of David"? What would this have called to mind for Joseph?

- Though Matthew doesn't explain anything of its significance here, Jesus' virgin birth made it possible for Him to be both fully human and fully divine. His father, in essence, was God, through the work of the Holy Spirit; His mother was the fully human woman, Mary. As fully God, Jesus was able to pay the eternal penalty for our sins (v. 21) for which finite humanity could not atone. As fully human, He could be our adequate representative and substitutionary sacrifice.

02. Matthew explained that "Immanuel" means "God is with us." What does this phrase teach us about Jesus, and why are these things important?

- By referring to Joseph as "son of David," the angel reminded Joseph of his messianic heritage.

03. What do we learn about Joseph from verses 24-25? What must he have believed about Jesus?

- The church in every age should recognize here a clear affirmation of Jesus' deity and cling tightly to this doctrine as crucial for our salvation. At the same time, Matthew emphasized that Jesus, as God, is "with us"; deity is immanent—fully present in our physical world.

04 . When the wise men arrived in Jerusalem, Matthew said King Herod and all of Jerusalem were "deeply disturbed" (v. 3). What likely caused their reaction?

- This was the consistent reaction of people to Jesus from His birth to His death.

- Herod was also certainly concerned that as an appointed king, the coming of the true inheritor of the Jewish throne (Jesus) could cost him his title and position.

05 . Look up Micah 5:2-4. What does this tell us about Bethlehem? About Jesus, the Messiah?

- Matthew's quotation of Micah 5:2 answers Herod's and the Magi's question regarding the place of the Child's birth while showing the city once despised as now honored. It also shows the Messiah will not only rule but also "shepherd" the people of Israel. A shepherd as an image of a ruler of God's people appeared commonly in the Old Testament. It implies guidance, pastoral care, and a sense of compassion.

06 . How did the wise men respond to seeing Jesus? Why?

- They were "overjoyed beyond measure" (v. 10). Have the group reflect on the joy they experienced when they first encountered Jesus. The overwhelming joy of Christ is always available to us when we focus on and worship Him with authenticity and faith.

07 . Why do you think the wise men presented Jesus with gifts? How were their gifts connected to their worship?

- Their worship of Jesus involved gifts of gold, frankincense, and myrrh. They presented these gifts to Jesus because He is a King worthy of such extravagance.

Apply The Text

08 . Both Herod and the wise men had essentially the same facts about the star and the Messiah. Why is intellectual information not enough to cause us to embrace Christ? What else is needed?

09 . Where do you see God at work revealing His plan for redemption in the world today? What role do you see yourself playing in this work?

10 . Jesus' birth shattered religious and cultural barriers. How does He still do this today?

leader guide
session 2

Focus Attention

What are some things you do in order to better identify with someone who is not like you?

- To identify with someone, you have to ask questions and listen. To connect with someone who is different, you must be genuinely interested and curious about that person because you don't live in his or her world. Jesus, actually did live in our world and took on the same human nature we possess. In identifying with us, Jesus demonstrated His profound love for us.

Explore The Text

ASK A VOLUNTEER TO READ MATTHEW 3:1-17.

01. What does it mean to repent? Why did John urge people to repent?

- Repentance is a confession of sin and a change of direction. When we repent, we admit that we have done something and we resolve to live a life of righteousness.
- Repentance was urged because Jesus was on His way, and those who would inherit the kingdom would be those who repent and believe (Mark 1:15).

02. When John told the Pharisees and Sadducees that reliance on Abraham was not enough, how did he point to Jesus?

- The Pharisees and Sadducees relied on their heritage for salvation instead of having a true faith of their own. As God is able to make sons out of "stones," He is able to bring Gentiles into the family of God. He does this through Jesus for all mankind.

03. Why do you think Jesus insisted on being baptized? Why did John hesitate?

- Baptism represented repentance, yet Jesus was sinless. John recognized his own worth in the presence of the Messiah and tried to discourage Jesus from being baptized. Jesus recognized that His baptism was an outward affirmation of His commitment to God. By being baptized, Jesus also identified with the people who were flocking to John in the wilderness.

ASK A VOLUNTEER TO READ MATTHEW 4:1-7.

04 . Why do you think God's Spirit led Jesus into the wilderness at the very beginning of Jesus' ministry?

- Jesus' experience might very well serve as a model for our own. A spiritual baptism led Jesus to a spiritual battle. The life that most pleased God was a life full of spiritual and physical battles and challenges.

05 . Jesus' first temptation is in verse 3. In your own words, what did the devil tempt Him with? What did the devil say about God? How do we face something similar?

- The devil challenged the belief that God provides for Jesus' basic needs. We too face obstacles that lead us to question God's provision. We don't have to waste time trying to turn stones into bread—we the Bread of Life.

06 . In the second temptation, the devil challenged Jesus to jump off the temple. Why was this a temptation for Jesus?

- This was about testing Jesus' faith. If Jesus jumped and sent angels to catch Him, He would have visible and experiential proof of God's faithfulness and love. But Jesus quoted Deut. 6:16—we don't need to test God's faithfulness.

ASK A VOLUNTEER TO READ MATTHEW 4:8-11.

07 . The third temptation involved Jesus being seduced with power. How was this an effort to circumvent God's plans and authority?

- Satan attempted to give Jesus all power and splendor apart from the cross. Satan insinuated that Jesus wouldn't need to go to the cross in obedience to God in order to have power. Jesus resisted by quoting Deuteronomy 6:13.

- Jesus stood strong against Satan and continued to the cross. Jesus was given not only all power on earth, but all power in heaven as well.

08 . How does the temptation of Jesus help us understand His identity?

- Jesus faced temptation as a human, just like we do. Jesus sympathizes with our struggles and weaknesses. Jesus demonstrated that He was also perfect, therefore qualified to pay the price for our sin. He gives us power over sin.

Apply The Text

09 . Think about some people in your life who need to be told about Christ. Pray for an opportunity to share with them the truths found in this study.

10 . What can you learn from Jesus that will help you face temptation in the future?

11 . How can being involved in a regular study of God's Word help you recognize and deal with temptation?

leader guide
session 3

Focus Attention

List stories and movies that include an unexpected plot twist. What makes a plot twist so entertaining?

- A plot twist can bring a sense of depth and realness to a film. It is more realistic, as our own lives rarely go as expected. In our study, we are going to look at Jesus' interaction with a man who unexpectedly had an incredible amount of faith.

Explore The Text

ASK A VOLUNTEER TO READ MATTHEW 8:5-7.

01. Look at the picture Matthew painted in verses 5-6. What was unusual about this situation?

- A centurion is a professional soldier who would have had in his command about one hundred soldiers. Being a Roman and a soldier, he wouldn't likely be quick to seek help from a Jewish civilian. His pleading shows vulnerability and humility.

- In Luke 7:1-10, we read that the centurion sent people to speak to Jesus on his behalf. There is no contradiction here, as a messenger carrying a request from the centurion would be speaking for the centurion.

02. While the centurion's response unusual, Jesus' response would have been culturally unusual as well. Why? And why was Jesus willing to help?

- Jewish leaders would usually want nothing to do with the Roman occupiers, and most of Jesus' ministry was concentrated among the Jewish people.

- Jesus was willing to heal the servant because of the urging of the Jewish elders, as the centurion was a good man. The humility of the soldier is important, as James 4:6 says, "God resists the proud, but gives grace to the humble."

ASK A VOLUNTEER TO READ MATTHEW 8:8-9

03 . What does the centurion's response reveal about this man's understanding of Jesus?

- The centurion said he was unworthy to let Jesus come into his home. In verse 9, the centurion revealed that his insight as a soldier gave him a unique perspective on Jesus and His authority.

04 . What does Jesus' willingness to go to the centurion's home help us understand about how Jesus valued people?

- Jesus would not let ethnic or political divisions keep Him from being about His kingdom work. We, too, should not allow any boundaries to keep us from reaching out to all people with the love and grace of Christ.

ASK A VOLUNTEER TO READ MATTHEW 8:10-12.

05 . What should we make of Jesus' response to the centurion's remarks?

- Jesus was amazed at the response of the centurion. It brought Him great joy to see someone believe in Him with such faith. We should understand this to mean that if we want to please Jesus, we should be people of faith.

06 . Why was it a big deal that Jesus said what he did about a Roman centurion? What can we learn from this about who we should strive to point to Christ?

- Jesus let the people around Him know that ethnicity doesn't equal godliness; faith is what matters. Some viewed themselves as a part of God's family because of their heritage and not because of their faith in God.

- Jesus is the King of people from all around the world. This should challenge us to focus on cultivating a true faith in Jesus and not rely on religion.

ASK A VOLUNTEER TO READ MATTHEW 8:13.

07 . Jesus demonstrated His authority through the healing of the centurion's servant. What might this mean for our lives?

- Those who don't have faith, but rely on religion like some of the Jews here, will not be a part of the kingdom. We gain eternal life and a relationship with God by faith, not by works or religion.

Apply The Text

08 . How should knowing that Jesus has authority over all things (nature, people, the future, etc.) change how we think of Him? How we live?

09 . Think about some areas of your life where you are struggling to recognize Jesus as the authority. What would it take for you to express your dependence on Him in those areas? What keeps you from taking those steps?

leader guide
session 4

Focus Attention

Why did Jesus tell so many stories? What does that tell us about Him?

- Matthew presented Jesus as a master Teacher who used stories to present important truths.

- Those who desire to be a part of Jesus' kingdom need to be able to understand what the King teaches.

Explore The Text

ASK A VOLUNTEER TO READ MATTHEW 13:1-9.

01. What do these verses reveal about Jesus' heart for people?

- Jesus saw a great crowd gathered and wanted to share with them God's truth and the realities of His kingdom.

- As Christians, we should cultivate that same desire for all people to know God's truth.

02. How did the story relate to the people who heard Jesus that day? Why was it important for Jesus to help everyone present identify with one of the soils in His story?

- People in all four categories would have been present when Jesus told this parable. As the Son of God, He would have known the spiritual condition of every person present and who related to which soil.

- Jesus helps us define reality by painting pictures for us.

03. What warnings did Jesus issue through this parable? How do the warnings given relate to Jesus' identity as the Messiah?

- Being a follower of Christ is more than an emotional experience. It also involves growing deeper into the truth of God.

- We should be aware of that which causes us to take our eyes off of Christ and resist those things. He alone is worthy of our devotion.

04 . What should we make of the varying amounts harvested in verse 8? What does this reveal about Jesus' value for all people?

- • Our value before God is based on who Jesus is and our union with Him by faith. Our desire should be fruit. We can't always control how fruitful our efforts will be, but we should desire to be fruitful.

- • God wants to use us and work through us. We must be willing to focus on God and our place in His kingdom.

ASK A VOLUNTEER TO READ MATTHEW 13:10-13.

05 . What was Jesus' reason for using parables? How did the use of parables serve Jesus' greater purpose?

- • Jesus explained that He taught in parables so that those who were willing to believe could understand the truth—while at the same time, those who were unwilling to believe might have the truth concealed.

- • Jesus desires for us to come to Him in true faith, with the right motives—not for self-centeredness or to puff ourselves up with pride in spiritual knowledge.

06 . How does Jesus' response to the disciples' question point to His authority as the Son of God?

- • Jesus knew the response of those with whom He shared since He is the Son of God. That knowledge did not negate Him giving them the opportunity to reject Him as the Messiah. God loves all people, even those who reject Him.

ASK A VOLUNTEER TO READ MATTHEW 13:14-17.

07 . How did Jesus' use of parables fulfill Old Testament prophecy? How did Jesus' use of parables confirm His identity as the Messiah?

- • Jesus quoted Isaiah 6:9-10, indicating that the disciples had just witnessed the fulfillment of what Isaiah prophesied.

- • Jesus fulfills all Old Testament prophecies about the Messiah.

Apply The Text

08 . What is the gospel? How might telling a story help you communicate the gospel to people?

09 . How might we help and encourage one another to share the good news about Jesus with the people around us?

leader guide
session 5

Focus Attention

Which of these terms is the most impactful on you personally: mocked, forsaken, or sacrificed? Explain.

- Jesus had been betrayed and arrested, prosecuted in a series of unlawful trials, declared guilty, then mocked and beaten. He was led away to be crucified.

Explore The Text

ASK A VOLUNTEER TO READ MATTHEW 27:41-44.

01 . Of those who mocked Jesus, who surprises you most?

- The crowd, including chief priests, scribes, and elders, mocked Jesus on the cross.
- Even the criminals being crucified alongside Jesus mocked Him.

02 . In what ways were the crowds' taunts and mocking wrong or unfair?

- Led by the religious leaders, the crowd mocked Jesus and challenged Him to have God "rescue Him" (v. 43). The crowd quoted Psalm 22:8, taunting Jesus. They were unaware that in doing so they were fulfilling prophecy about the Messiah.
- The crowd taunted Jesus saying "He cannot save Himself" (Matt. 27:42), when His death was actually providing salvation for all who trust Him to be saved. They called for Jesus to "come down now," when the only way to secure salvation for all was for Him to stay on that cross until dead.

ASK A VOLUNTEER TO READ MATTHEW 27:45-49.

03 . What is the significance of the supernatural events accompanying Jesus' death?

- As Jesus was dying on the cross, God covered the land with darkness in the middle of the day, allowing nature to reveal the supernatural power of Jesus.

- Both physical and spiritual darkness filled the land during this time.

04 . How did Jesus' words reflect His anguish? The pain of sin? His separation from the Father?

- Jesus quoted Psalm 22:1. In that darkest moment, Jesus carried the crushing burden of the world's sin and felt separated from the Father.

- Matthew records only this one of Jesus' sayings from the cross. The remaining six are found in the other three Gospels (see Mark 15; Luke 23; John 19). The crowd misunderstood Jesus' words, thinking He was calling on Elijah the prophet for relief.

ASK A VOLUNTEER TO READ MATTHEW 27:50-52.

05 . Matthew noted that Jesus gave up His spirit. What does that mean, and why is it important for us to understand?

- Jesus was sovereign throughout the crucifixion, controlling even the timing of His death. He gave His life as an offering for us; it wasn't taken from Him.

06 . What events marked Jesus' death? How would you interpret the significance of each event?

- The temple curtain was torn from top to bottom. There was an earthquake that split the stones. "Saints" who had died were raised from the dead.

- Jesus' death occurred at 3:00 p.m., the same time as the afternoon sacrifice at the temple. The priests would have been present in the temple to witness the tearing of the curtain. The torn curtain symbolized sinners' new access to God with the barrier between God and humans removed.

- With the earthquake, God showed that something amazing had happened. With the resurrection of the saints, God promised to one day raise us.

07 . How should we live in light of Jesus' sacrifice for us?

- If we have never asked forgiveness for our sins and placed our trust in Jesus, we can do that today. As believers, we should live each day so that our words, attitudes, and actions reflect that Jesus is the Messiah and Lord of our lives. We should live with thankfulness for the sacrifice Jesus made through His death, so we could have an eternal relationship with God.

Apply The Text

08 . With your group, list ways of testifying that Jesus is the Messiah. What can we do as individuals? What can we do as a group?

09 . Take time to reflect on your life when you were separated from God. What image from the crucifixion best illustrates your life at that time?

10 . Consider the changes that have happened in your life as a result of what Jesus did on the cross and your trust in Him. How has He changed your heart and character?

leader guide
session 6

Focus Attention

Have you ever witnessed a car accident or crime? Were you asked to report what you saw? Why is eyewitness testimony so important?

- In most situations, the best, most accurate information will come from people who actually saw the event happen. In today's session, we will study the account of those people who were eyewitnesses to the resurrection.

Explore The Text

ASK A VOLUNTEER TO READ MATTHEW 28:1-4.

01 . What is significant about who discovered the empty tomb?

- Mary Magdalene and "the other Mary" were named as the first visitors to the tomb. In that culture, women would not have been viewed as trustworthy witnesses, yet Matthew included them as important eyewitnesses to the resurrection. All people are valued in God's kingdom.

02 . How does the reaction of the soldiers demonstrate the power of God's glory?

- The angel of the Lord appeared, as in other key biblical moments (see Ex. 3:2; Matt. 1:20; Acts 12). God's glory can overwhelm even the most confident people.

ASK A VOLUNTEER TO READ MATTHEW 28:5-10.

03 . What evidence of the resurrection do we see in these verses?

- The angel reported the resurrection, reminding the women that Jesus had promised this would happen. The angel invited the women to see for themselves the evidence of the empty tomb.

- As final confirmation of the resurrection, the women met the risen Savior as "they ran" to tell His disciples the great news.

04 . Why is it important that we not delay in obeying God?

- The more we trust God, the quicker we will respond in obedience to His plans for our lives. Delayed responses to God's prompting may cause us to miss out on opportunities to serve Him.

ASK A VOLUNTEER TO READ MATTHEW 28:11-15.

05 . What were the motives of the chief priests as they devised their deceptive plan?

- If the resurrection is true, perhaps Jesus was who He claimed—the Son of God. The chief priests couldn't risk this potential threat to their position and authority.

- The chief priests devised a plan to bribe the soldiers to say Jesus' disciples stole His body while they were sleeping. But if the soldiers were sleeping, how could they know it was Jesus' disciples who stole the body?

06 . What do most people think about the resurrection of Jesus today?

- The women heard of Jesus' resurrection and rejoiced. The priests heard of the resurrection and rejected it by telling a lie to discredit it. People are faced with the same choice today. We must either accept it or reject it.

- Some who reject the resurrection simply ignore it, thinking it irrelevant for their lives. Others deny it as being absurd or unbelievable. Still others reject the resurrection because they want nothing to do with Jesus and His claims in their lives.

ASK A VOLUNTEER TO READ MATTHEW 28:16-20.

07 . How did seeing the resurrected Christ change the disciples' view of Jesus?

- Seeing Him resurrected, the disciples had no doubts as to Jesus' true identity. They were eyewitnesses to the gospel, knowing that Jesus was alive and that all who trusted in Jesus would share in His resurrection.

08 . How is the command that Jesus gave tied to His resurrection?

- The resurrection showed the power of Jesus and proved that He was the promised Messiah. The promise of Jesus' power provides His followers with the needed confidence to complete the task assigned to them by Jesus.

Apply The Text

09 . How does Jesus' resurrection give hope?

10 . What role does worshiping Jesus play in your weekly schedule? What adjustments do you need to make to be more involved in worshiping Him?

11 . Think of some people in your life who have not yet accepted Jesus and the truth of the resurrection. How can you lovingly challenge their views and talk to them about the hope you have in Jesus?

notes

notes

notes

notes

notes

notes

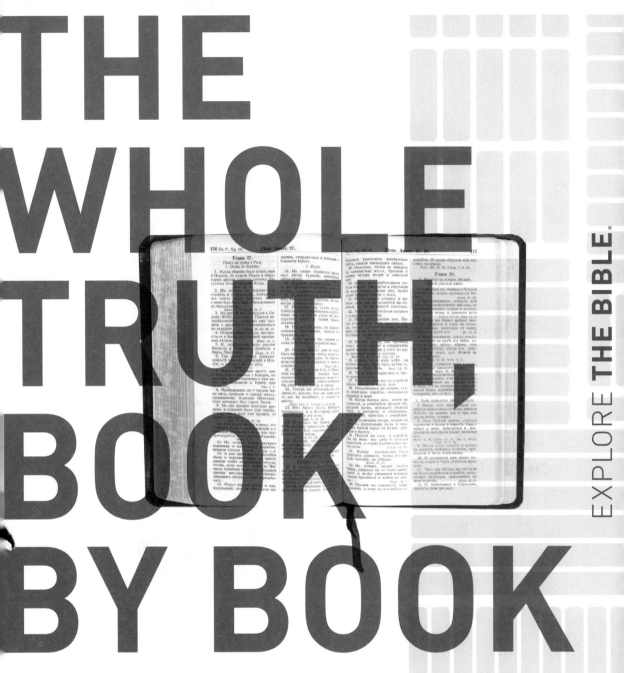

THE WHOLE TRUTH BOOK BY BOOK

When you Explore the Bible book by book, you give students the whole truth of God's Word. Each Bible study session frames Scripture with biblical and historical context vital to understanding its original intent, and unpacks the transforming truth of God in a manner that is practical, age-appropriate, and repeatable over a lifetime.

Download a free sample at
goexplorethebible.com/students

EXPLORE THE BIBLE

FOR STUDENTS

WHERE TO GO
FROM HERE

We hope you've enjoyed learning about some of the characters of the Bible. Don't miss the next volume in this year-long study, *Characters: Volume 6: The Followers.* This study focuses on the lives of some of the earliest followers of Jesus and their impact for His kingdom.

For more information, call 800.458.2772 or visit: lifeway.com